To Grandad George

ACKNOWLEDGMENT

I was proud, honoured and privileged to play football for Mayo in all grades from underage right through to senior. As I've written in this book, the shirt was always much more than just a piece of cotton.

It symbolised and stood for so much more.

It carries history, prestige, and expectation... and as players who wear it, we are merely carrying the flame, making sure that we set proper standards that are carried forward into future generations.

I know that I didn't get everything right during my career. There are incidents that I regret, of course there are.

But playing for Mayo was all that I ever wanted to do as a sportsman. That dream of winning an All-Ireland senior football title drove me on. But it wasn't just me.

The men I soldiered with felt the same. Kenneth, Trevor, Dillo, Chuckie, Zippy, DB, Austy, Hartey, Clarkey, Heaney, Nallen... to name but a few!

I'm just sorry that we didn't get over the line. In the 2004 and 2006 All-Ireland finals, we happened to run into a Kerry juggernaut on both occasions.

The central section of the book is the 2006 All-Ireland final, through my eyes. Watching the game over and over again on DVD brought back a litany of memories and the decision to introduce some of the characters who were there with me brought up so many stories and anecdotes... some make me smile and others are just how it was.

Jackie Cahill helped to piece the jigsaw together and I thank him for his assistance.

My fiancée, Sara deserves a special word of thanks. She's been incredibly patient and loyal throughout the entire process.

I love you, Sara.

My family has been there for me since day one. To my parents, Carmel and Frank, thank you for your unconditional love. The same applies to my sisters, Tara and Elaine, and my brothers, Frank and Kenneth and Trevor.

Kenneth and Trevor know what it's like to pull on that shirt too. They know what it feels like to line out on All-Ireland final day and they've felt the pain of defeat. But they had their good days as well.

More good days than bad.

I certainly believe that to be the case with my career. I'm proud of the fact that I'm Mayo's all-time leading scorer but that may not be the case forever. Thanks to the lads at home in Shrule for their nurturing and in latter years, to the guys at Parnells in Dublin for taking me in like one of their own. There were good times at college too, first at Dublin City University and later University of Ulster, Jordanstown. Declan Brennan and Niall Moyna were terrific to me at DCU, as were the academic staff at UUJ.

I've dedicated my book to Grandad George.

He brought me everywhere when I was young but passed away just a week before the 2006 All-Ireland final. I wish we could have done it for him on that *One Sunday* but I know that he was proud of what I did and what I achieved. Granny Evelyn, too, and my extended family members.

It's fair to say that there's been colour and controversy along the way. My senior Championship debut was in 2002 against Galway and that was a day I'll never forget... for the wrong reasons.

A decade later I decided to call time on my county career, prematurely. I had my reasons for that. I believe that I've outlined them clearly in this book.

Some day, Mayo will win the All-Ireland again.

Those years of hurt will be washed away and I hope that I'm there to see it. It will be that *One Sunday* that young boys like me dreamed about kicking a ball around the back garden.

But for now, take a step back in time with me.

Conor Mortimer,
October 14, 2014.

ACKNOWLEDGMENT

'ONE Sunday: A day in the life of the Mayo football team' is a book with a difference.

The middle section is devoted entirely to Sunday, September 17, 2006, when Mayo played Kerry in the All-Ireland senior football final.

Conor Mortimer was one of the Mayo forwards on that fateful day and he brings us on an intimate journey into All-Ireland final day and all that goes with it.

Conor's experiences over that weekend mirror that of Mayo football since their last All-Ireland senior win in 1951.

We begin to understand the hopes, fears, burning desire and almost crippling expectation.

It is a wholly honest book and through Conor's eyes, we are provided with a unique insight, from a player's viewpoint. Thanks to Liam Hayes and Hero Books for helping to create the vision and for helping us to follow it through to conclusion.

A number of characters are introduced and reintroduced throughout the middle section and consequently, this book is not only Conor's experience of the All-Ireland final, it is also the experience of his teammates and mentors.

I first met Conor in the noughties and found him to be an immensely likeable character.

I now consider him to be a true friend and this project is one that we have spoken about for a number of years.

I remember 2012, when he decided to walk away from the Mayo panel. It was a decision that he did not reach lightly and I hope that the content of the book bears that out. As the old saying goes, there are two sides to every story and how he has explained it to me made perfect sense.

As we wrote this book, there was many a long night and in this regard, the patience of our fiancées Lisa and Sara is much appreciated.

Lisa and I are getting married in a few weeks and that is a day that I am very much looking forward to.

Lisa, I love you very much and for your constant patience and support, I thank you.

To Lisa's family, a heartfelt thanks also. Resilient, resourceful and strong-minded people...I warmed to you instantly.

Thanks to Conor's parents for the photographs from his early years. Cover photographs and match photographs were supplied by Sportsfile. I have also been fortunate to get to know Kenneth and Trevor, Conor's brothers. Two great guys.

To Damian Lawlor and Colm Keys, thanks for helping me along the way. Your feedback was invaluable. To my childhood friends, including my groomsmen, James and Iver, college buddies and the other great people that I have met along the way, thanks for having my back over the years.

My father, John and mother, Angela have been a constant support to me and for their continued, unconditional love, I thank them. I am extremely proud of my siblings, my sister Rose and brothers, Brian and Andrew (the other two groomsmen!). All are doing well in life and God willing, that will continue to be the case for many years to come. Much love to you three, your partners, Richie, April and Aoife, and baby James, my first nephew.

Finally, a light went out in my life in November 2002, when Derek passed away. He continues to inspire me to this very day. Sleep well, pal.

Jackie Cahill
October 14, 2014.

CONTENTS

PROLOGUE

Sporting debuts are meant to be days that you'll never forget. The first rung on the ladder, the opening page of the scrapbook. It's supposed to be the hat-trick of goals for the Premier League striker at a new club, the professional golfer who lands that Major at the first attempt, the young kid on the block who comes through and takes the inter-county scene by storm.

Mine was different. I had my front teeth knocked out, missed a free from 25 metres at the end, and copped a head-butt in a local pub later that night. My senior Championship debut for Mayo was against Galway in Castlebar. June 2, 2002. A Connacht semi-final with 24,800 spectators packed into McHale Park.

I'd come into the game in a rich vein of form. My National League debut season had gone well. My League bow was against Down in Ballina and I kicked five points from play. Not a bad way to start. And the big tallies kept on coming – 1-8 against Clare, including two points from frees. Five points in the Sligo game, 1-6 against Cavan, including three frees, seven points against Derry. And four more points when we played Fermanagh.

As the season progressed the stakes and intensity levels rose but I still managed six points against Tyrone in the League semi-final in Enniskillen in April. We found ourselves on the wrong end of a 0-11 to 3-12 defeat but up against Conor Gormley, one of the finest young defenders in the game at the time, I was pleased with my contribution. I had an idea that Championship would be a different kettle of fish but the sheer scale of it took me by surprise.

Our manager was Pat Holmes, a former player with Mayo who had played in the 1996 and '97 All-Ireland finals. He played alongside my brother, Kenneth in the Mayo defence and just 10 weeks after sitting in the dressing room for the 1999 All-Ireland semi-final as a player he had taken over as manager.

Pat was a young manager cutting his teeth at the highest level but eager to learn. He would win the National League title in 2001 and I will always be grateful to him for bringing me into an extended panel for winter training. It was tough going on those cold nights in Tourmakeady but I felt at home right from the start. I was a confident young player and believed that I could have slotted into the team straight away but two winters of pre-season training prepared me for the step up.

Now the biggest test of my career was upon me – a senior Championship debut against Galway in Castlebar. And I was nervous before throw-in. There was a different feeling in the dressing room. I was togging off alongside my brothers, Kenneth and Trevor and other established inter-county players such as David Heaney, David Brady, Gary Ruane and our goalkeeper, Peter Burke.

Galway were All-Ireland champions and my marker, Kieran Fitzgerald was an All Star from the previous season. Fitzy was from Corofin, a tall, strapping lad. He was over six feet tall and in the mood to teach a young forward still wet behind the ears a thing or two about county football. It wasn't long before I was given that harsh introduction to the big time.

There was a ferocious dunt as I made my way into the corner before throw-in. A little later a stray elbow from another Galway player as I went for the ball left me with blood pumping from my mouth and a dental bill to settle after the game.

Fitzy was like that. I found him awkward, all arms, but he was a good footballer and a difficult opponent to get past.

I managed to kick four points, split between play and frees, but my contribution to the game will be remembered for a missed effort right on full-time.

Standing over a free from 25 metres out, shooting into the South or Albany end of the ground, I connected pretty well but the ball tailed wide. A score then would have put us ahead at a crucial juncture but late points from Pádraic and Tommie Joyce saw Galway home by 0-12 to 1-7.

It was a harsh introduction but I thought I was ready. It had been a good day until then, with neighbours and extended family members calling to the house from early in the morning to wish us luck. I visited my grandfather, George and I was really looking forward to the day that lay ahead, and the endless possibilities. I tried not to over-think and to focus on the positives.

I deserve to be here... this is my stage, I told myself.

And the prayer that George taught me... "Jesus, Jesus... Help Me."

It wasn't long after my 20th birthday. And the anxiety was unlike anything that I had ever experienced before. Because I'd never felt like this at any time in my football career, I wondered if there was something wrong with me? I guess it was a case of getting the first ball into my hands and going from there.

Fitzgerald was a challenge but I'd studied him before the game. It's a practice that continued right through my career, right to this day. I'd ring other players that would have marked defenders I'm coming up against, or I'd scan local newspapers for information on them. When I was young, George had loads of videos in the house – the VHS ones that you don't see any more. I was always looking at players on the Mayo team, forwards to learn from, and defenders... to see where they were strong or weak. So when I got into training with Mayo, I could use my knowledge, play well and get on the team.

That was the plan.

I saw that as my homework before I joined the Mayo senior squad. When I went to training then, I wasn't naïve. It was a huge leap forward and while nothing can fully prepare you for it, at least I had something of a head start... in my mind.

No matter how well you play for your club, when you come in with the big boys they're so far ahead in terms of experience and mentality. Cuteness is the word I'd use for it. Running in a straight line for a ball, turning and sticking it over the bar isn't as easy at county level as it with the club. Senior county players are the best in the county... or the country even! And so I'd watch videos of Galway's Pádraic Joyce, Kerry's Maurice Fitzgerald, Peter

Canavan from Tyrone, guys who were the very best in the business. Just to see how they did it.

Joyce is my favourite player of all time. I watched him playing club football quite a bit for Kilererin and some of the scores he took were breathtaking.

I believed that I could skin Fitzy… if I got a good supply of the ball that I liked – low, and coming to me at angles.

But if the ball came in high, he was the favourite to gobble it up. I remember the first score that I kicked from play, watching it just clearing the crossbar. It was one of those where you think the goalkeeper is about to catch it but it scrapes over. A lot of my scores were like that.

Will it… will it?

Just about.

Later in my career, kicking a free would equate to a point from play for me! Sometimes there's a lot more pressure kicking that difficult free, from a static position, as I would quickly discover. I've had frees to level games with ferocious pressure weighing on my shoulders. Some people will remember the one that won us the 2006 Connacht final against Galway. But I remember Kevin McStay writing about the 2001 Hastings Cup final, when we beat Tyrone at Under-21 level. It was the same kind of free from an almost identical angle.

Alone with my thoughts.

Ball in hand…

… the outcome of the game down to me… alone!

But on this big day, on my Mayo Championship debut, I missed.

I let people down.

Photographs I viewed later of me lining up the kick show just how worried I was. I wasn't happy with my boots either… Adidas Predators at the time.

No excuse.

I was wearing them because they were cool and in fashion, but they weren't right for me.

And if you haven't got the right boots on when you're kicking, you're in big trouble. They're the tools of the trade. I look at players now and they have no tongues in their boots.

The new Predators, for example, don't have them. But I always need a tongue in my boot, so that I'm not kicking the ball on my instep and hurting myself.

I'll get an extra 10 yards on a kick with a tongue in my boot. And I still have boots that I'd have worn as far back as seven or eight years ago, because they feel just right.

I think I might have misjudged the swirling breeze into the Albany End. Lining it up, I curled the ball... looking to drift it in.

It was a kick I'd nailed on countless occasions, because McHale Park was a pitch that I knew well. As I kicked the ball, the breeze changed direction but I still couldn't believe when the ball went wide.

It was a poor miss.

The Joyces tagged on those couple of scores and that was that. One strike and we were out of Connacht, even though the back door was there for the All-Ireland series. The missed free really annoyed me. I should have converted it, no doubt. But experience would tell me that missing or converting a free is dependent upon a number of factors – the environment you find yourself in, your opponents, your mentality, the stage of the game.

The skill is the same but when skill and emotion collide, it's not plain sailing. When I returned to the dressing room, that's when the magnitude of it really hit home.

I buried my head in my hands but my teammates were brilliant. Heaney and Brady patted me on the head and told me not to worry about it. My mouth was hurting bad too. There was no dentist on call on a Sunday but we still managed to source one. My top four middle teeth were broken to the gum. I don't think the repair job was as good as it could have been because I've had a lot of work done on my teeth since.

The Mayo county board settled the bill and a dental bridge was required to replace the missing teeth. I hadn't remembered my mouth being particularly sore during the game but it was killing me afterwards. I went to the sideline to take a drink during the match and it was pointed out to me. I only realised how bad the damage was when I visited the dentist later.

The boys went out for a few drinks down town when I was finished in the dentist. Rocky's in Castlebar was the popular post-match haunt. The lads wouldn't stick together so much in one big group, more spread out around the pub.

I perched myself down the back, beside the DJ box.

I was in the place less than five minutes when I made my way to the toilet. I was met by a guy who told me that I was the reason Mayo had lost. He planted me with a head butt, straight between the two eyes.

And that was that.

I got upset and left Rocky's.

If I get hit, my response is to become emotional inside. I won't show it publicly but later, I'll release on my own. The upset was borne out of embarrassment. I remember the pub being packed but the assailant got away with it... as far as I know.

I didn't even tell Trevor.

I retreated to a B & B where I was staying and didn't leave my room for the night. I cried that night, and eventually managed to get some sleep.

PART ONE
In The Beginning

CHAPTER 1

THE boundary between Mayo and Galway lies on the edge of the village of Shrule. The Black River divides the two counties and serves to split two Gaelic football strongholds. I'm told that the ancient Gaelic name for my home village was Sruthair, which translated means river or stream.

Nestled between Ballinrobe in Mayo and Headford in Galway, Shrule is roughly 16 miles from Galway city. There's one primary school there, where I spent some of my formative years, and while most students from my area attend the Presentation College in Headford I was an exception.

I was born in Galway University Hospital on May 23, 1982. I'm the second youngest in the family, older than my sister Tara. Frank is the eldest, ahead of Elaine, Kenneth and Trevor. Frank was supposed to be the best in the family as a footballer. But Frank enjoyed himself when he got older, lived in England for a while and has worked in the quarry for the last 15 years. Elaine's a teacher at St Gerard's in Castlebar now and Tara's moved to London, working for Tesco.

Our house was tiny, so small that Trevor would later move out to live with my Grandparents, George and Evelyn, who lived a five minute walk away. If you walked in the front door of our house when I was a child, a large room on the left housed one of those big old Amstrad computers. The wall was lined with boxes containing sports gear for the children, and the Amstrad was perched on Dad's desk. This was his room for work purposes.

The kitchen and sitting room merged into one, with a kitchen table and a range for heating. Patsy Donnellan was our next door neighbour, and on the other side was an empty house once owned by a Captain Martin, an old war veteran.

Captain Martin had passed away and I used the front door of his house for target practice, kicking a ball from across the street. The windows of the house were broken and while the Gardaí would call looking for offenders, we were never caught.

As a young boy growing up, soccer was the sport I loved. I quickly developed an affinity for Liverpool Football Club, badgering my mother to buy me the latest team kits when they hit the shops.

Behind George and Evelyn's house I imagined that the back garden was Anfield, Liverpool's home. I built my own goalposts and the nets were big and square, like the ones used at the 1994 World Cup in the USA.

Granddad George, who passed away shortly before the 2006 All-Ireland senior football final, hailed from close to Westport but he was well known in our local area because he ran a shop. As kids we loved Granny and Granddad's house. It had a loft out the back where all the stock was held, and we used the toilet rolls to recreate the scenes from the World Cups when they would be thrown on the pitch.

I was always kicking a ball around and slept with one every night until I was 13 or 14 years old. I'd always have to have the latest model from the English Leagues… Mitre or Adidas branded. And I'd pray for a wet day so I could skid a new ball along the turf behind my grandparents' house.

I loved watching the spray as the ball thudded into the back of the net.

When I got older two big sticks got me started on my homemade USA '94 goals. I took a pole from the local GAA pitch, dug a curve into the top of the timber posts and balanced the new crossbar on top. Netting was secured in Glencorrib… old torn nets, and the job was completed by tying the netting back to the trees in the garden.

The call went out to my friends and they'd bombard me with shots. I was a goalkeeper when I was young and David James was the Liverpool goalie at the time. Soccer remained a big part of my life until I was 20 years of age, and James was such a big hero of mine that I took his surname as my Confirmation name. As well as playing juvenile Gaelic football with Shrule, I lined out for the local Riverside Celtic soccer club and later with Galway outfit, Mervue United. But I realised that if I was to have any hope of making it in the big time as a professional footballer, which was very much a pipe dream, I'd have to give up Gaelic football. I did have trials with Swansea City as an Under-14 player and underage International scouts took a look at me but sacrificing Gaelic football wasn't something that I was prepared to do.

Lunchbreak in national school was the time for us young lads to hone our developing skills, and when school was over for the day it was a case of getting home as quickly as possible, munch down the dinner, and get outside for more football.

My father, Frank and mother, Carmel had their hands full trying to look after all of us. Frank took a chance with his business, buying a plot of land to get started. He was in NUI Galway at the time, a few months away from becoming a qualified doctor, but he veered off in this new direction.

During the good times, business was brisk but it's a lot more difficult nowadays, since the downturn. But Frank's business, set up in the 1980s, is still alive.

We were happy as kids even if we didn't have an awful lot, as the old saying goes. But Dad worked hard, probably too hard, and we wanted for nothing. What used to annoy me was seeing my friends' parents buying big cars, but my folks had a more simple philosophy and outlook on life. Whatever would do the job would suffice. No point buying a new car if you already had something that could take you from point A to point B.

Any pocket money was likely spent in the chipper across the road from our house, where I used to hang out quite a bit, playing the old style arcade games. We had a hideout at the back of the chipper, and before I was old enough to join in this was where Trevor and the older lads used to knock about.

If the younger boys went near the hideout they were in danger of a few digs. Trevor's crew was Darren Murphy, Donal Gibbons, James Martin, Ciaran Walsh, David Walsh and James Lohan. I used to pal around with Lohan too and that helped me to become a full member of the hideout.

There were three pubs in the village – the Highway, Gibbons' and Craddocks. When I was older, I liked to knock in there on the night before the game. I'd spend an hour there, drinking Miwadi and chatting with the locals. I've never been a great sleeper and that was a way to pass the time.

Shrule was your typical rural village and the real hive of activity was Galway city, where people used to go for dinner, the movies and nights out.

I spent a fair bit of time in Tuam too, visiting my grandfather, Frank Acton and my uncles on my mother's side. Frank was a useful footballer in his time and won a Galway SFC medal with Tuam Stars back in the 1940s. I'm led to believe that he played alongside Frank Stockwell, who is renowned as one of Galway's greatest ever players.

In primary school, I had a sensitive charm about me, cheeky yet innocent. There can't have been any more than 20 pupils in my class and while Paddy Joe Dooley ran a good ship, I could never really relate to teachers. I saw them as figures of authority, hierarchical, and I didn't like that. That outlook continued throughout my school years. I resented people in positions of authority and sport was my release. I was never academic, but I tried to be the very best that I could be with a ball at my feet or in my hands.

I was an okay kid in general, I think, but school just wasn't my thing. I was a poor student and it was only in recent years that I realised that I could apply myself academically when I put my mind to it. I'd have been okay at maths and spellings in school but I never paid enough attention to the various other subjects. I ached for break-time when we could get out and play soccer and football. I loved when the school would play a match away from home because it was the chance to simply get away from the place for a few hours.

All that I needed was ball, boots and a pair of gloves. Dad worked hard to make sure that all of us had the sports gear that we needed, as he mined the quarry in Beclare. He had played football and hurling at St. Mary's secondary school in Galway himself and Granddad George played a bit too in his day. I was told that Dad was a useful player and so too was my uncle Austin.

George was the biggest influence on my early years. When Dad was working, George would bring me to training sessions with the local Shrule club and to matches. And when I started in the Mayo school of excellence as a young teenager, it was George who ferried me to and from training. He'd sit in the car waiting for me to finish, reading the paper. It was a rite of passage in many ways because he'd done the same for Trevor and Kenneth.

George had more time on his hands to look after us like that. Dad often worked from six o'clock in the morning until ten at night. We had a shed down the back and I'd go down there most evenings, messing about with the trucks and ending up covered in grease.

Dad was there almost every day and it seemed to me that his life was a neverending cycle … work, home, bed… and do it all again the next day. Even now he should be retired but he can't drag himself away from the business. He knows nothing else.

And he's a survivor. It was tough for a while when the crash came in recent years because a lot of the money that had been made was used to keep the business ticking over in the quiet times. But it's not long before any disposable cash is used up because diesel has to be bought, machines need fixing and staff have to be paid. Because Dad isn't selling as much as he used to, business is a slog.

Trevor was involved too but he's left the country because work dried up. He's in Mauritania now and sending home some money to help keep the business here afloat. Mauritania is a country in the Maghreb region of

Western North Africa, a tough place to be but Trevor hopes to be back home some day, for good. He's out there, earning a crust and when he returns he'll have a head start in Ireland. He was right to do so because the reality is that you don't make money in Ireland now in the quarrying game.

When the time came for me to leave Shrule national school, my parents decided that I would become a boarder at St. Mary's College in Galway. I hated it there and I resented them for sending me. I might have had a 10 per cent interest in school, at a push, but being sent to St. Mary's meant that figure dwindled to zero.

I cried my eyes out every night for the first two weeks at St. Mary's. A look out the window presented a stunning view of Galway Bay, but I wondered what I was doing there?

The way for me to survive at St. Mary's was to immerse myself in football. My goal was to make the school's senior team by Junior Cert. That would see me pitting my wits against some of the best up and coming young players in Connacht.

And I also knew that there were some perks associated with being on the school team. There were half days for matches and if you're playing with the school team it's a bit like being a college footballer in the United States. You're looked at differently... at least that's how I felt, and you don't tend to get as much hassle.

And yet that feeling of loneliness lingered on an almost constant basis. I was away from home five days a week and yet home was just a 20-minute drive away. What made the situation worse was that my friends were in Headford secondary school, which was closer to Shrule. They went to school every morning but got home every evening too. And looking through that window at the city killed me. There were nights when I knew that the lads at home were training with Shrule. I was with Mayo underage teams and that was once a week but my mates could go home and watch TV in their own house.

Maybe my time at St. Mary's toughened me up but it's not something that I've ever thought about, or wondered whether it shaped me in any way. The one message that I took from my time there is that I will never send my kids to boarding school, if I'm fortunate enough to become a father. My parents thought that they were giving me a chance at a better education by sending me to St. Mary's but I had no interest, even though Trevor was there too.

Football kept me going and two of the teachers at St. Mary's were Sean Óg de Paor and Liam Sammon, the former Galway footballers. I didn't have Sean Óg for any subject but I was well aware of who he was. At the time Sean Óg was a well known defender with the Galway senior football team, who would emerge to win All-Ireland senior titles in 1998 and 2001.

It was only really in later years that I got to know Sean Óg. But I remember the homecoming in Tuam for the victorious 1998 Galway team. There was never a jealousy thing there with me as far as Galway were concerned. They won those two All-Irelands in that spell and good luck to them.

I never had a hatred for Galway, just a gee-up when I was playing against them. And I can even say that I'd know a few of the Galway lads better than some of the Mayo lads. I'd have great time for my all-time hero, Pádraic Joyce, but also Michael Donnellan, Tommie Joyce, Nicky Joyce, Michael Meehan, Kieran McGrath and Kieran Fitzgerald, who marked me on my senior Championship debut and left me with that bloodied mouth.

Boarding was tough, very tough. I didn't really feel vulnerable or exposed because I kept myself to myself. And I knew that Trevor was there and if there was any hassle, he would sort it out fairly quickly. Trevor was a strong boy, even back then. And he was my protection from some of the punishment that gets dished out to the younger kids in boarding school. A few of the lads in my class were well able to look after themselves nevertheless. And, unfortunately, some of them went down the wrong road, ending up in prison and suffering with drink and drug problems.

I never felt in any danger of ending up like that because I was always so keen on football. And I didn't take my first drink of alcohol until I was 22 years of age. I'm the same now as I was back then, very single-minded about football. Even my fiancée, Sara thinks that I'm a pain in the ass because I think and talk about the game so much.

The time came for Trevor to leave St. Mary's and that made me edgy. Thoughts constantly ran through my head.

I don't want to be here.

I'm done here.

No more. .. no way!

The priests would come in at night-time, shining torches to see if we were asleep. It felt like prison. To me, that's what boarding school was. I told my parents how unhappy I was. They didn't like to hear that but their stance didn't change. I was going to school and that was it. I argued with them that I should have been in Headford, with my primary school friends Ronan Walsh, Dermot Geraghty, Kevin Walsh and Cian Donnellan.

My Gaelic football career progressed steadily in spite of this. I wasn't strong enough at the time but I could score when I had the chance and I picked up the ball with some space to work in. I was playing minor at 14 and 15 years of age with Shrule. I also played senior Championship football with St. Mary's and I'll never forget my first game in Athenry, against Roscommon CBS.

Stephen Lohan was playing for the CBS and he was good friends with Trevor at the time. It was a huge game, pissing rain in Abbeyknockmoy. I played well and scored a few points but we were beaten. Unfortunately I didn't win anything of note with St. Mary's but the learning gained from my time there was huge.

I met people that I still keep in touch with but it was just everything about the place that got to me, even the food. Discipline was strict but while some of the priests gave me a hard time, I got on well with most of them. One particular priest was in charge of study time and I got caught listening to an English soccer match on my Walkman.

I was tuned into BBC Radio 5 Live on a crackly reception and my Walkman was confiscated. One day, I was in the priest's room to pick up something or other and I started mooching around in there. Rumour had it that a cupboard existed with a stack of Walkmans that had been taken from other students. Hey presto! I found them! I felt like Robin Hood returning them to the lads they'd been taken off.

Steal from the rich and give to the poor!

I wasn't a troublesome student but I was always up for mischief. I'd get in trouble for arriving back late to school after a wander down town.

It was a five-minute walk into the city from St. Mary's and while my hurling career can be summed up very quickly, the game did get me into trouble on one occasion. I had a bad grip on my hurl and needed to find a new one. To leave the school, I had to sign out at 4.15 p.m. and sign back in within an hour.

Off I went into one of the sports shops, Roche's, to find myself a new grip. I put five or six in my pocket but as I went to hightail it out of the shop, I was nabbed by the security guard.

He was fine about it once I handed back the grips, but I ended up late back to St. Mary's.

It was tea-time and if you were late back the priest would look at you and demand an explanation. I made up an excuse and he went mad.

'Don't lie to me!' he boomed.

It was Fr. Joe Delaney and I was grounded for a week. I learned a lesson there and then – don't lie to a priest.

They'll forgive you, one way or another.

Sometimes mothers are not so forgiving – and one particular priest incurred her wrath after I was given a clout. I told Mam what had happened and up she marched from Shrule, and banged on his door. I never found out what happened after that!

We attended mass every morning at St. Mary's and prayer-time was every morning and evening. The routine was… get up at 7.30 a.m. shower, down to church for eight, prayers until 8.20 a.m. and then breakfast until 8.50 a.m. Class began at 9.10 a.m. and school ended at 4.0 p.m.

From 4.0 until 5.30 p.m. we were off and tea-time was from 5.30 to 6.0 p.m. Study was from 6.15 until 8.0 p.m. A break until half 8.30 p.m… and then back to study until 10 p.m.

So, you can guess how unhappy I was with my life dissected by a clock.

***

My dislike for the place grew with the onset of acne.

I had loads of spots and I was freaked out by them. I was constantly rubbing my face. I was convinced that if my face was smooth it was okay, but I was rubbing it so much that it became one red patch. But it was smooth and that's all that mattered to me. Upstairs, I'd pick and squeeze the spots.

Blood everywhere but eventually my face was smooth. It was obsessive behaviour. I tried everything but Clearasil didn't work and there was no solace either from visiting skin specialists. The spots weren't just confined to my face. They were all over my body, but particularly bad on my face. They looked like craters on my skin. Acne affected me to the point where I didn't want to go out.

Shower time was another chance to get at the spots. Blood everywhere again but I'd wash myself off and feel fine. Out to the mirror for another look and another attack on my skin.

My diet didn't help me. Mam would arrive with sweets, crisps and bars most evenings, and breakfast was eggs and beans. We'd have chips every evening for tea, with more beans and sausages. I'd go to the shop for lunch, crisps and rolls. I longed for Friday evenings, to get home for the weekend.

It always broke my heart going back on the Sunday nights. George would drop me at the gate, with tears in my eyes and he knowing that I was upset.

What could he do?

It got to a stage where I even resented George.

Surely he could tell Mam and Dad how upset I was and get me out of here? Four long years I spent at St. Mary's but I finally got out of there. St. Jarlath's in Tuam and the prospect of a Connacht colleges title was too loud a call to ignore. My parents were finally realising how unhappy I was at St. Mary's and came around to my way of thinking.

Either move me to St. Jarlath's... or I was leaving school!

That was my ultimatum.

CHAPTER 2

St. Jarlath's College in Tuam boasts a long and rich tradition of Gaelic football excellence. The Hogan Cup is presented to the All-Ireland college winners and while St. Jarlath's have not lifted the trophy since 2002, a haul of 12 titles remains a record to this day, four clear of St. Colman's of Newry.

I'd like to say that the goal of achieving a good Leaving Certificate was my motivation for leaving St. Mary's for St. Jarlath's but that would be a lie. The sole reason for going there was to play football.

St. Gerald's College, Castlebar and St. Colman's, Claremorris, have also achieved provincial and national success, but St. Jarlath's was just 15 minutes from home and an ideal fit.

Going there also ensured that I had escaped the boarding school experience of St. Mary's. I could come home in the evenings, knock around with my mates and sleep in my own bed. George was there again to drive me to and from school. He'd leave me at the front gates in the morning and pick me up every evening.

But as soon as George was gone, there was many a morning where I'd chuck my bag inside the gate and meet up with Nicky Joyce and Diarmuid Blake, two lads who went on to play senior for Galway.

We'd often go down the town and pass the hours in the Abbey Tavern, slotting our pocket money into the pool tables.

I was forever dodging classes but that didn't bother me in the slightest. After St. Mary's, this was one hell of a release. Evening time was all about football. I could train with the club and I was doing well with Mayo's underage teams.

Life was good, my football was improving and I had targeted a Connacht Championship with St. Jarlath's.

Thankfully, the target was in sight as we had a fantastic team. Blake and Joyce were there and so was Michael Meehan, one of the most gifted Galway footballers of recent times. We also had John O'Shaughnessy from Westmeath and a young Ciaran Murphy, the former Newstalk radio reporter, who is now part of the *Second Captains* TV team.

St. Pat's were next door to us and they had good players too, like Galway's Kevin Brady and Michael Comer. The two schools are amalgamated now but St. Pat's had a tradition all of its own. Known then as Tuam CBS, they would win three Connacht Championships – in 1980, 1989 and 1995. But the current provincial roll of honour sees St. Jarlath's well out in front with no fewer than 48 Connacht titles to their name.

I enjoyed my year there, although there wasn't much study done.

I did the bare minimum to get by, just enough to pass my Leaving Certificate. What was of far more importance to me was the fact that I was now making a name for myself as a footballer. And being part of a successful St. Jarlath's team was the next rung of the ladder.

I was now starting to really trust my ability. I was already a junior footballer with my club at the age of 16 and I loved those battles with guys much older than me. In so many ways I believe that being exposed to that level of competition and physicality at such an early age allowed me to play for as long as I did. I'm not the biggest, as people can see, but when I was introduced to weights in later years, I was able to lift pretty heavy.

I didn't really worry that my lack of height would come against me.

I was always known as the proverbial nippy corner forward. People would have said that I had a good pair of hands but I was never confident under a high ball. I won't even go for many of them because I don't have the confidence to catch them.

In any case, I always preferred the more forward-friendly ball. It should be at least 60-40 in favour of the forward but you'd find in club football that it's 50-50 at best. At St. Jarlath's we had players capable of delivering the kind of ball that forwards thrive on.

And when the 2000 Connacht final rolled around I was buzzing for it. Our opponents were St. Colman's College from Claremorris and I knew that they didn't have the players or the class to touch us. I remember being in the dressing room before the game, urging my teammates to feed me the ball. I would do anything to win this game and the prospect of a Connacht medal was huge to me. All of my friends who went to Headford didn't have one and the fact that we were up against a Mayo school provided added motivation.

We won the game at Tuam Stadium by a cricket score, 2-18 to 0-2. The *Irish Independent* match report described me as "outrageously talented" and while that might be extreme, I did have a good day. I finished the game with seven points, including five frees, and the newspaper article reckoned that I had the potential to be the best Mortimer yet.

"Either he is set up for the greatest fall since Humpty Dumpty, or he will mature into a stunning talent."

I'll let you be the judge of that.

We had played St. Mary's in the Connacht semi-final and that, naturally enough, was a tough outing for me. I took no pleasure in beating my old school, who had a very decent team themselves that year. But I felt that if I wanted to become a Connacht colleges medal-holder, St. Jarlath's was the place to be. Winning that Connacht title in 2000 fully justified my decision.

I was still into the soccer too, in a big way. And I have to admit that as a sport, I'd prefer soccer. You have that bit of time on the ball but Gaelic football is different, all rush... rush... rush.

You can't really enjoy Gaelic football as an adult player, like you could as a youngster. You could take the piss out of defenders but I tend not to engage in the verbals any more. Perhaps it's maturity, but when I was younger I had more of a cocky demeanour about me. I knew when I had the measure of an opponent and I'd let him know all about it.

'I'm after scoring again... what are you going to do about it?' It wasn't the nicest thing in the world to say but I was young then and didn't think a second time about it.

By then I was a member of the Mayo minor squad and this was a natural progression as I'd participated in the school of excellence from Under-15. I remember that a lad by the name of Rossa Higgins, from Claremorris, was with me at the start. I rated him as good, if not better than me at that age. But the amount of young players that fall away from the game is huge. They're not given the right advice, not looked after or coached properly. Each individual player has different aspects of their game that they need to work on. Not every defender is the same and the same applies to forwards.

I wasn't great for taking direction when I was younger, I must admit. What I heard a lot was that I had to pass the ball more and bring other people into the game. I didn't think that I had to, because I was scoring and that was my outlook until into my 20s. I needed to score, too, because I was very much a confidence player.

And I loved taking frees because if you pop over a couple early on the confidence builds. I always think that it's a difficult situation if a team has two recognized free-takers. One is racking up the scores but the other may be suffering because not only is he missing out on some of the handy frees, he might also be struggling from play. He'll struggle to make an impact because he's not getting those handy ones. If, for example, you tap over a couple of early frees and add two from play, suddenly you're up to four points.

That's good for confidence, good for you and good for the team. That's why I practiced so much – I always wanted to be on the frees.

I took a lot of my advice from my brother, Kenneth. He was hugely successful when he played and he instilled confidence in me from a young age.

I respected him massively because of what he had done on the field himself. I see a lot of coaches and managers out there now who have never played the game.

It might just be me, but I find it difficult to listen to somebody who has never been there and done that. You might argue that the soccer coach, Jose

Mourinho never played at a high level and neither did some of the managers that I played under for Mayo. But Mourinho is tactically astute and studies the game.

The top football coaches will put in hours and hours of study, potentially to find a fault in an opponent. I don't know if there are many Gaelic football coaches who would watch a video of a player during the off-season, to find out what he needs to work on.

Too often they'll rely on their own judgement or intuition, and this is a flawed process. A manager might have a selector or statistician telling him how many balls a player has turned over during a game, but does the manager know how well the player is moving or if any physical imbalances exist in his make up?

I read a story once about David Beckham when he was at AC Milan. The medical director at the club, Jean-Pierre Meersseman, claimed that fixing one of Beckham's teeth helped him with his running and balance. That's in-depth analysis of an individual player.

Players and managers think that commitment is training, doing your extra bit, watching what you eat and sacrificing the social life. And that is huge commitment, I'd agree, but you can still go the extra mile. When I played, my entire life was Mayo football… drinking water… icing an injury at work… always doing whatever extra thing that needed to be done in order to be ready to play.

It remains the case for many players, but not enough players are ticking those boxes. I still practice, even as a club player. You need that confidence going into games, that knowledge that you have the work done. It's not enough to go the gym on a Monday, train Tuesday, get back into the gym on Wednesday, and train Thursday.

All of this preparation really doesn't amount to much if you can't go onto the pitch and kick the ball over the bar when required in a game. I've seen Mayo players of recent times kicking some awful wides, and I know that if they practiced more on their own that wouldn't happen. If you practice enough on that weaker foot, for example, the ball still might not go over the bar but it will be a damn sight closer than the previous effort when the ball was probably sent horribly wide.

***

The work I'd done before that Connacht Colleges final stood me in good stead for the game. It was a great win for the team but on a personal level, I was extra proud. It was great for the family as well... it was a big medal to have in my possession! And the victory was a massive boost to my self-confidence. I was good at football but I still had the bad skin... the acne.

Football was my escape and I could play.

On the field, I was doing things that I wouldn't be particularly proud of now but I put them down to the innocence of youth. As I've already admitted, I'd yap at my direct opponent, take a score off him and start yapping again.

'Is that the best you can do?'

It was non-stop chat.

I imagined that I was the great Kerry player, Pa Laide. He was a flying half-forward and he'd use his speed to get into scoring positions before kicking the ball over the bar. I was so confident in my own ability that I began talking to the media as a minor player. You don't know any different then and you don't choose your words as carefully as you might now. I was never briefed about that kind of stuff but I had a *name* from a young age. I still hadn't won an awful lot until that colleges success with St. Jarlath's, but I was also a member of the Mayo minor panel that later reached the All-Ireland final of 2000. It's a regret of mine that my minor inter-county career consisted of just one season.

And it was my mouth that was a big reason for that.

Early in 1999 I'd travelled to Australia as part of an Ireland Under-17 International Rules team. I was called up on the back of good form for Mayo during our successful run in the Ted Webb (Under-16) Connacht Championship.

I was playing at wing forward and selected by John Tobin, the former Galway footballer who managed his native county and Roscommon. Shortly after we returned home from Australia, we played a minor league game against Galway. I was marking Michael Comer, who was also a member of the International Rules panel in Australia. I was chatting away to Mikey during the game. He was a lad from Corofin that I knew. We would have played against each other at school as he went to St. Pat's in Tuam.

Cathal Hennelly, one of our selectors, roared in at me to shut up and, of course, I wasn't slow about replying. I never heard anything from Mayo management after that incident... not for the rest of the year. They reached the All-Ireland final under J.P. Kean but lost to Down in Croke Park by three points.

I could only presume my verbal altercation with the management on the sideline was the reason why I was overlooked for the remainder of the year. I marked Rory Keane twice in club games that summer, scoring heavily in both, and Keane was in the half back line on the county team.

Still no call... and that hurt me.

There were three Shrule boys on the panel, Ronan Walsh, Kevin Walsh and Dermot Geraghty – and I was heartbroken watching them head off to county training. Presumably the management felt that I was too big for my boots but what disappointed me was that they really didn't know anything about me, because they didn't ask me back in after the Hennelly incident.

I watched that All-Ireland final from the Canal End. But my form was too good to ignore in 2000. I had that Connacht colleges medal in my back pocket and my form was excellent. In the Connacht Championship I scored one of the more bizarre goals of my career.

I received the ball early in the game and went straight for goal, scything through the middle of the Sligo defence. We were playing into the scoreboard end at McHale Park in Castlebar, and I had noticed that the Sligo goalkeeper had ventured too far to his right and was literally standing at the goalpost.

That left me with a wide open goal and from between the 45-yard line and the D, I let fly. It looked like a great goal but it really wasn't. The goalkeeper had left an opening and I went for it.

We went on to win the Connacht final against Roscommon and that set up an All-Ireland semi-final against Westmeath in Croke Park. I missed a penalty in that game, skying the ball over the crossbar. I'd aimed for the top corner but got underneath the ball and over it went. Paul Prenty scored a last minute goal to rescue a draw before we came through a really tough replay against them in Carrick-on-Shannon.

Our opponents had been five points up at half-time in the drawn match and they also dominated the first half of the replay.

At half time they were 0-4 to 0-2 ahead but we started the second half really well and got level within three minutes of the restart. We went two points clear but Westmeath rallied again in front of a 7,000 attendance.

But we got a break when Westmeath midfielder, Padraig Leavy was sent off for a second booking and with five minutes remaining I managed to win a free, and convert it... to put us a point clear. We clung on for a 0-7 to 0-6 win and I finished the game with four points to my name. That was a good Westmeath team we had beaten and one of their scorers on the day was PJ Ward, who would later go on to play for Offaly.

Our All-Ireland final opponents were Cork and, while I kicked six frees, I was well marked in that game and could only marvel at the talent that was the Cork forward, Conrad Murphy. He scored a point from underneath the Cusack Stand side shooting into Hill 16, and another from the 14-yard line tight on the touchline – two of the best scores that I ever saw in Croke Park. Watching Murphy doing his stuff, I was envious. That should have been me landing those gorgeous scores and propelling our team to glory.

But in the *Big House* that is Croke Park, losing All-Ireland finals would become a recurring theme.

CHAPTER 3

THE message came from the sideline that I was coming off with nine minutes left against Limerick in the 2002 All-Ireland senior football qualifier at Dr. Hyde Park.

I'd scored four frees but manager Pat Holmes decided that my race was run. I wasn't best pleased because it was a tight game and I still felt that I could contribute something down the home stretch.

I decided to head straight for the dressing room but I was headed off at the pass by one of the backroom team.

I walked towards the touchline and as I made my way back to our bench, I could feel the *red mist* descending. I whipped off my jersey and threw it straight in over the dugout.

I was fuming but this was an act of petulance that I regret.

I had no idea that what I had done – an act borne out of sheer frustration – would create such a storm. I was soon accused of disrespecting the Mayo jersey but it wasn't meant like that at all.

I could have done things differently for sure, but I was young and didn't think of the potential consequences.

To be honest, I didn't think that there would be any fallout. I certainly wouldn't do it now but to be labelled as a guy that had shown blatant disrespect to the Mayo jersey hurt me. I had worked so hard to get to this place in my career and yes, I had flung the shirt into the crowd, but I knew that the jersey was much more than just a piece of cotton. It symbolised and stood for so much more. From that point of view, what I had done was wrong.

It was a stupid mistake.

And with hindsight, I didn't need anybody else to tell me that.

The story became a big deal and Denise Horan, a journalist working for the *Western People* at the time was on my case. She rang me for a comment and I argued that what I had done was nothing to do with disrespecting the Mayo jersey.

I told her that players don't train five days a week unless they have total respect for the jersey... for the Mayo cause.

But the abuse still came thick and fast, and it was a valuable lesson for me. I began to understand that a man paying a tenner in at the gate doesn't just gain entry to the ground... he's also entitled to fire a volley of abuse at a player if he sees fit.

And at tight provincial venues or club grounds, I always heard the smart remarks from the stands and terraces. I hear some players talk about how they're so focused on the game that they don't pay any heed to what's being said. I wasn't like that. I didn't like it, but I tried to use it to my advantage.

Perhaps that jersey episode marked me out as a troublemaker from the start. There were isolated incidents over the years, like the time when I was out in Galway after a game.

Some of the other Mayo lads were in a nightclub and I went to Supermacs for something to eat. A group of lads attacked me and, when word spread, Trevor came out of the nightclub and was hopping mad. I was sitting in a car with Fr. Charlie, a priest from Tuam who would always keep an eye out for us if there was a game on earlier in the day and we were out socialising.

Trevor got involved in a ruck, and I got out of the car to help him.

I was arrested.

As I sat in the station, I could hear a group of Mayo lads outside.

They were singing...

Free the Mayo one.

It was an uncomfortable experience.

I didn't do myself any favours with my reputation as something of a boy racer. A Garda that I knew from Galway pulled me over one night in Dublin when I was out for a drive. I was in a Subaru Impreza and while the Garda didn't really say anything to me, it was still hassle.

There was another night when I was driving the Subaru in Galway, with Alan Dillon and James Gill in the car. A Garda stopped me and asked if I had been drinking? I was asked to provide a breath sample, but the machine wasn't working.

The Garda then told me that a reading couldn't be taken and that I'd have to come back to the station.

'What about my car?' I asked.

'One of the Gardaí will take it back to the station.'

'No way...!' I replied.

'You're not insured to do that,' I told him, but I was left with no option. I went with the Gardaí in their car and left Dillo and James in my one.

'You'd better hope that you weren't drinking,' I was warned. Back at the station I blew into the machine and it provided a zero reading.

'Are you happy now?' I asked him.

It's silly stuff when I look back on it now. Maybe it was the hair and the attitude that made me an easy target, and maybe they were the same reasons why I got one serious hiding in Castlebar. I was out with a few boys from home.

I went to the toilet... and next thing six or seven lads set upon me.

I curled up in a ball.

I later discovered that the attackers were guys from Castlebar and Breaffy, but I never did find out why they did that to me that night.

I'm not providing these examples to portray myself as some kind of hard case. Because I wasn't. I'd rather steer clear of hassle than actively seek it. I wanted to be known as a good footballer more than anything else, and that

2002 season had steeled me for the years that followed.

I wasn't innocent all of the time, of course.

After the 2008 Championship myself and Andy Moran sat down for an interview with the *Mayo News*. The following curve ball came my way.

'Some people would feel that Mayo will win nothing with you on the team... that you're not a team player! What would you say to them?'

That was the question.

In rapid-fire self-defence I said the first thing that came into my head.

'They'll win nothing without me either!'

I had given a smart answer.

It was a silly comment, and one that I'd regretted very quickly.

Again, it comes back to a point that I have made earlier... players, particularly when they're young and in the public eye, need some media training.

But what I needed most of all in order to play well was a large dose of confidence. When the crowd is with you, your confidence is sky high and you play better. Whether it's a gem of a point or laying off a good pass... you know the crowd is behind you... you hear them... and then... bang... you're away.

That's how a lot of players get their adrenalin – from the crowd... from the people in the ground.

When things weren't going my way, I worked harder, practiced more. I lived by the work I did. If I played well, it was because I had been practicing three or four times that week. When I kicked the winning free against Galway in the 2006 Connacht final it was because I'd probably kicked 100 of them the night before in Castlebar.

The big part of the reason why I wanted to play for Mayo was Kenneth. He was such a good defender, wore the jersey with pride and rarely, if ever, let the team down. Invariably he'd mark one of the best players on the opposition team, guys like Vinny Claffey from Offaly, Kerry's Mike Frank Russell or Joe Brolly from Derry, and usually he'd get the better of them.

When I was young, Kenneth left Shrule to play with Claremorris at club level. He lived there and worked for the bank. We had been relegated and it made sense for Kenneth to play senior football with another club.

I remember a game he played against Crossmolina in Charlestown. Kenneth and Ciaran McDonald had a tremendous battle. McDonald was a serious player but Kenneth marked him out of the game and I felt so proud. He was like Steven Gerrard to me – untouchable on the field. He won two All Star awards at right corner back in 1996 and '97.

I never really spoke to him about the impact of losing All-Ireland finals but I could see it in him that 1997 hurt him more than the previous year. The day before the '97 final, I asked him if they were going to win on the Sunday?

He was in no doubt that we would. It didn't work out like that, as Kerry's Maurice Fitzgerald produced a brilliant performance and I felt sorry for that bunch of Mayo players because they put everything into it. What always struck me about them was how tight they were.

In our time, you might have 12 or 13 lads hanging out together after a game, drinking pints, but Kenneth's crew could swell to 20. It was different back then, and not uncommon for them to go for a couple after a training session. That practice has completely died out now but the drinking was certainly heavier than it is now. With the application of sports science and greater awareness of an athlete's body, footballers nowadays know they wouldn't get away with it.

The training that Mayo team went through with John Maughan in the mid-90s was savage. Maughan put them through the pain barrier. Running... running... running until they could do no more. They might have had to crawl but they'd still get over the line.

And that's why they had no fear in games.

The boxes were ticked.

As a result, from watching them, this also became a trait of mine during my career. I always felt that if the work was done and your direct opponent got the better of you, there was no reason to feel bad... you just came up against a better player on the day! But if you missed out on a session, got lazy and then ended up being toasted in a game... that was a problem!

There's no room for excuses.

Too many teams and players nowadays look for the cop out.

If you train 100 per cent on Tuesday and Thursday and do the extra work that's require, you have no reason to feel bad, even if the team is beaten by 10 points on a Sunday. But if – most especially at club level - guys are missing one or two nights of training and not putting in the work, that can also be the reason why a team will lose by 10 points.

I always consoled myself with the knowledge that I had the work done. Unless a defender marked me out of the game, I wouldn't have played badly. And there were plenty of times when I was marked out of matches while still learning my trade. Physically, I wasn't that big. I relied a lot on skill, speed and elusiveness. Kenneth wasn't particularly tall either but he was a terrific corner back.

I used to mark him in training and his awareness of where to be when the ball arrived was frightening. If you scored even a point on Kenneth you'd be doing well. He was tough, a great bit of stuff.

Trevor was more of a forward but he had a problem with shooting. He was never the greatest shooter but he was an imposing physical specimen, built like the proverbial brick s***house without ever lifting massive weights. Trevor made his senior inter-county debut two years before I did.

I had to suffer my hard winter training for two winters before coming on board with Mayo.

Holmes had brought me into an extended training panel before I made the breakthrough, to soak up the experience of being involved with such an elite set-up.

I was still a minor player but training with the seniors was a magical thing. The winter training sessions in Tourmakeady were gruelling.

Poor lights.

P****** rain.

And running… and running… and… running.

Granddad George would drive me there and Maurice Sheridan would drop me home to Shrule on his way back to Galway.

Maurice would be chatting away in the driver's seat but it was going in one ear and out the other. I was living the dream and, while I wasn't playing games, I was training with the Mayo senior football team. For a young lad that was hard for me to get my head around. Still, I'd be sitting at home while the seniors were playing matches and thinking that I should be there, because I always had confidence in my own ability as a developing player. I was playing well in training, too. I was young and small, but taking the big hits from the likes of David Brady and Fergal Costello hardened me up.

I'd always try to avoid Costello because he trained as he played. There were no half measures with 'Cos'.

There was no real adjustment period when Pat Holmes picked me for a first league game in Ballina against Down. I banged over scores straight away. I was also kicking the frees right from the very start, as Maurice Sheridan was unavailable in 2002.

I was light, but the game was different then. Players weren't as bulked up or conditioned as they are now. Nowadays, we see young players coming through from underage with a history of weight training already behind them.

The runs were savage and the hits were hard. Heartbreaking long runs – different to what teams are doing now, that's for sure. But I liked that soreness the next day. It was a good soreness – it confirmed that I'd trained hard the night before.

If you weren't up for those crippling long runs back then, you were told to go home. Simple as that. Nowadays, if a player isn't fit, he'll get extra training or be given diet advice. Mollycoddled, to an extent, to get the player to where the management want him. The fitness that we were looking for back then was difficult to attain. You had to do your extra bit on your own, unregulated to a large extent compared to now.

It was character forming stuff, but nothing beats experience and the 2002 season provided me with plenty of it.

There was that missed free against Galway, for starters, busted teeth and a head butt from a stranger in a pub. The morning after that game was horrendous when I awoke in that B & B. I bought the papers and my feeling of guilt increased. I hadn't gone out to lose the game for Mayo. It was a bad miss but you win as a team and lose as a team. No one player can lose a game because there are so many twists and turns over the course of 70 minutes.

That experience taught me to really enjoy the victories over Galway that followed. Because losing to them really hurt, more than losing to any other team. And beating them felt good... really good.

I grew up as a Galway fan to a large extent but I soon began to understand the rivalry that exists between the counties. I played in so many big games against them and experienced the other side of the coin as a supporter. Followers of a team need to understand that no matter what they're feeling, they can never experience the emotion that a player carries into a game - and the sometimes ridiculously high level of emotion that he must live with afterwards.

Fans are ecstatic, they go crazy but they return to their everyday lives and routines fairly quickly.

It's the players and management that are left to sift through the wreckage and pick up the pieces. I heard later that some kid, after the game against Galway, had kicked the ball over the bar from the same spot where I had missed. I didn't see it happening, but I also knew there wasn't a packed house shouting and roaring at him.

Something like that could break a young player, if he buys into it. I wasn't the only one, and I certainly won't be the last to have a stinker of a Championship debut. And you'll never play again if you buy into the post-match talk and the media chat. I resolved there and then to work harder and the fact that we still had a second chance in the Championship was some consolation. Losing to Galway saw us pitched into the qualifiers. Roscommon were out first opponents and we had home advantage again in Castlebar. We beat them by 0-20 to 2-8 and I scored six points, including three from play.

Mayo were back in business.

But the jersey episode would come back to haunt me, costing me my place on the team for our Round Four qualifier against Tipperary in Ennis.

As a player you can always gauge whether or not you're in line for a starting place on how the manager is interacting with you in training sessions leading up to the game. If he's talking to you, you'll play... but if he's not, you won't.

It's that simple.

He won't say 'great score'... if you kick a good point, for example. Holmes broke the news to me as I sat in my car after training. He leaned in.

'We're not starting you against Tipperary.'

'Why not?' I asked.

I didn't get a straight up answer but I suspected that it was a disciplinary thing, related to the jersey.

'I don't want to hear it,' I said... before driving away. We beat Tipp by four points to set up an All-Ireland quarter-final against Cork at Croke Park.

This should have been one of best days of my career – the chance to play at the stadium for the first time as a Mayo senior player. I came on in the 44th minute to replace David Tiernan. McDonald was on the bench too but he came on in the first half and scored 1-3. It wasn't enough as we bowed out of the Championship, losing by 1-10 to 0-16. It was Kenneth's final game in a Mayo jersey. And it was the last game in charge for Holmes.

I didn't feel any great animosity towards him and I was sad when he left because he had given me my shot. But the jersey incident became a big thing. I felt that he caved in under public pressure and it was the wrong kind of attention for me.

But I'll be forever grateful to Holmes for giving me the opportunity to learn and develop as an inter-county footballer. The 2002 season had provided me with plenty of football and life experience, that's for sure. Holmes inspired me but, as all players discover, managers don't stick around forever. It's a rare thing, too, for a manager to return for a second spell in charge of a county team.

But if there was one man who could return to lift our spirits, one man who could buck the trend and command instant respect in the dressing room... that man was John Maughan.

CHAPTER 4

JOHN Maughan was a man I wouldn't have known all that well on a personal level. I would have met him a few times during his first stint in charge, as Kenneth was one of the mainstays on his team at that time. I was one of the little guys hanging around at training sessions, watching, listening... learning.

I like Maughan and, to this day, he remains a good friend of the family's. As a manager he was a dominant figure and brought real personality to the role. He dropped me for the 2005 All-Ireland quarter-final against Kerry, for instance, but that was a decision I couldn't argue with. Otherwise, Maughan supported me as a player and, in return, he had one hundred per cent commitment from me.

With Maughan, you got back what you put in.

The harder you worked, the more game time came your way.

There were times when I played poorly and yet Maughan would pick me again the following week. And he always wanted us to be a mentally strong team. The perception has always been out there that Mayo are mentally brittle but Maughan set about changing this.

And he did that by putting us through the wringer at training. Maughan's backroom team included Liam McHale, George Golden and Martin McGrath. It was an impressive line-up and a management team certainly capable of taking us in the right direction.

Under Maughan we got fit… really fit. Some players wonder before they go out if they have the legs for the last 10 minutes but we could have played three games in one. We had so much belief in our fitness, and that was down to the savage running we were put through in Belleek and Ballina.

Belleek is like a big cross-country course. I ran cross-country when I was younger and it's a discipline that requires a strong state of mind. There was a mile of a loop and we were doing seven of those at full pelt, as fast as we could.

Do one.

Break.

Repeat.

Every second mile was coming back in the opposite direction, with a big hill to contend with.

Maughan drove us hard but we could have the banter with him too. He was flashy and flamboyant but very single-minded, and he never worried about what other people thought about him. With his army background, he didn't allow negativity to seep into his psyche and while I can only speak for myself, I fully believed that he was good for us.

He brought us to an All-Ireland final in 20004 when few expected it.

I was pleased to see him return because I knew what he had done with Mayo in the 1990s, and before he took charge of the Mayo seniors for the first time he had guided Clare to an impressive Munster final victory over Kerry in 1992. I wanted to play for Maughan and I wondered how he would make me a better player.

The big question was if Maughan could deliver the Holy Grail?

Very quickly he had us thinking 'Yes'.

He made us believe that we could do it. Anyone that wasn't prepared to commit one hundred per cent or stepped out of line, would not be tolerated.

That much was clear.

***

There were plenty of comments passed about his appearance on the touchline. Maughan was fond of wearing shorts and if it was a tracksuit, he'd have it pulled up to his pecs. That was just Maughan's way and nobody should underestimate how physically strong he is. I was in the gym with him a few times and he's an animal.

He loves work, and likes being a big dude.

On the social scene, he afforded players certain latitude because Maughan could party with the best of them. I remember one training session a couple of days after a match when we ended up in a nightclub in Castlebar. I think I may have fallen outside but Maughan heard about it and he smiled at me when we arrived into training.

'Had ye a good night last night?'

And when he asked that question, I knew what was coming next.

It would always be a massive physical session a couple of days after a night out. He knew that he was going to bury us and it was literally the case that only the fittest would survive under his regime.

Half an hour into Maughan's training, we were nearly all crippled. We could be on our 15th run... and there would be 20 lads *walking*. They just didn't have the legs for it.

The lads were walking... but what they really wanted to do was crawl.

Maughan challenged us in training, and on match days. He was a good motivator and had plenty of belief in our collective and individual abilities to get the job done. There was great balance in the management team, and of course training camps abroad went down well.

Those were opportunities to work hard and play just as hard. Monday to Saturday, we were out every night. Everyone was encouraged to socialise but no matter how bad the hangover was, you had to be up at eight o'clock the next morning. If you didn't get out of bed, you were *home*. One player didn't get out of bed for a day and didn't last too long on the panel after that.

It was Maughan's way of testing us. We were allowed to do pretty much as we pleased but training was compulsory.

I never struggled to get out of bed.

I'd look after myself the night before. The older lads were capable of having a good drink but they were experienced and could get away with it. The problem was that the younger cubs tried to keep up with the older guys and often ended up buried. Half an hour of training in the morning would have the drink pretty much gone from the system.

It was a top-class set up in Portugal, with ice-baths and the best of food. We'd always know too if Maughan and the other members of the management team were after overdoing it the night before. They'd arrive with the big sunglasses on them to hide their eyes from the glare of the sun.

Our National League Division 1B campaign in 2003 was a mixed bag. Seven games, four defeats and three wins. We finished against Fermanagh in Charlestown, losing by a point, and they were opponents that we would see again later in the season. Our stuttering form continued into the Championship and after getting past Sligo by three points in the Connacht semi-final, we were beaten by Galway. I was taken off with four minutes left at Pearse Stadium. The qualifier route lay in store for us once again and it was a short-lived journey.

At Markievicz Park in July, Fermanagh beat us by a point. This wasn't supposed to happen, but the rebuilding process began immediately and, 14 months later, I played in my first All-Ireland senior football final.

Not many, if any, expected us to embark on such a run. Certainly not me, as my National League game time amounted to 13 minutes as a substitute against Westmeath in our final game.

I missed the vast majority of the campaign after undergoing groin surgery. Something had to give, particularly after I had spent a number of months on painkillers. Difene was my drug of choice before I switched to Celebrex, a potent anti-inflammatory that I managed to source from a guy in England. What a tablet that was! It got me through, but one of the side-effects was stomach pain and I had no choice in the end but to bite the bullet and go under the knife of Gerry McEntee, the former Meath midfielder.

When I was in for my assessment with Gerry originally, Stephen Kernan from Armagh was also there. I always felt that Stephen didn't play for Armagh as much as he could or should have. He certainly wasn't as prominent as his brothers, Tony and Aaron and yet I would have rated Stephen as probably the best footballer in the Kernan house.

My groin operation was conducted at the Bon Secours hospital and I'll never forget chatting to an older guy sitting in the bed next to me, who had suffered a serious injury in a match. I was sure that I was having a full-blown conversation but my next memory is waking up in the ward after surgery. That was the first time I had ever had a general anaesthetic. I wasn't supposed to drive home after the procedure but being the stubborn fool that I was, I did anyway. If I kept my leg straight, it wasn't too bad but arching it any bit at all sent a darting pain into my groin.

What I had was a condition known as adductor tendinopathy. There are five hip adductor muscles and their main function is to pull the legs together. They're used quite a lot in sprinting and particularly in football. Injury can occur through overuse and presumably my problem was a direct result of me kicking so many frees from the ground. The groin suffered because I was compensating to an extent because of a serious injury to my left knee sustained in 2001, while on duty with the Mayo Under-21s.

I got back pretty quickly and Maughan was patient.

He didn't want me rushing back to play League matches just for the sake of it and I spent plenty of evenings at the local pitch in Shrule, running in straight lines. I couldn't twist or turn with my groin and there was one setback when I spotted a loose ball on the pitch one evening and drew a kick at it. I was in agony on the ground for what must have been half an hour before I rang Gerry McEntee.

'What did you do?' he enquired.

'Ah, I was walking around Gerry and… I felt this little pinch.'

But it was much more than a little pinch. I could feel myself ripping open. That put me back a week or two and pus began to build up on the scar left from the operation. That meant infection, but thankfully it cleared up and I got back into the swing of things again.

New York was our first port of call in the Championship and it was a thrill to be there, and to be in a bar in Times Square until one or two o'clock in the morning with my sister, Elaine, just killing time. She'd travelled down from

Boston and it was brilliant to catch up. The game itself provided us with few problems.

We racked up 3-28, and I managed 1-12. The Connacht semi-final pitted us against Galway again, and at McHale Park we beat them by 0-18 to 1-9. That was particularly pleasing after losing by four points to them 12 months earlier. Now we were winning by six.

A clear path had now opened up to the quarter-finals of the All-Ireland Championship and I collected my first Connacht senior medal when we beat Roscommon in the final. That victory set up a huge clash with Tyrone, the All-Ireland champions, at Croke Park. But this was a Tyrone team still coming to terms with the grief of losing one of their most inspirational players, Cormac McAnallen, to sudden death syndrome in March. Still, Tyrone were keen to honour Conor's memory by retaining Sam Maguire, and they were favourites to beat us.

The winning of that game was our midfielder, Ronan McGarrity. We spoke in detail about his role for two weeks before the game. If McGarrity stopped Sean Cavanagh playing, we had a massive chance. And our midfield was phenomenal for us. McGarrity scored a point, and David Brady had three more.

Fermanagh, a team we knew quite well by now, had made remarkable progress of their own and were our opponents in the All-Ireland semi-final. We were in big trouble when James Gill was sent off with 27 minutes left but we managed to get out of Croke Park with a draw, 0-9 apiece. I'd put us ahead in the closing stages but Fermanagh managed an equaliser. The replay was another one of those dogged games but we managed to get over the line with late points from Austin O'Malley and Trevor. People suspected then that we might not be up to it in an All-Ireland final. And that proved to be the case against Kerry in September.

They decimated us by 1-20 to 2-9. I received a watery eye early on and that finished me for the rest of the afternoon. We were beaten in every facet of the game.

Kerry were awesome.

We'd stayed at Finnstown House in Lucan the night before the game. It was just perfect, really quiet and a huge contrast to what we would experience in 2006, when we joined the queue for breakfast with Mayo supporters. I was 22 years of age when I played in my first All-Ireland final and the occasion passed me by. The day before the game, I was whizzing around the roads of Mayo in a Subaru Impreza that a friend of mine owned.

Red car, rocket of a thing.

There I was, bombing along the roads around Claremorris and Ballinrobe when Maughan rang.

'What the f*** are you doing?'

I'm not sure that I had an answer. It was hardly ideal preparation.

Kerry took full advantage of our inexperience. And if you go through their team from No.1 to No.15, they were probably one of the best that ever played the game. We were poor, admittedly, but Kerry ruthlessly exposed our weaknesses.

People in Mayo can clutch at straws and look for the *what ifs* and *maybes* but there were none. We were blown out of the water in 2004. Kerry beat us with football and they had such natural forwards. What I also admired about them was their refusal to deviate from the game plan. There was no plan B. If plan A wasn't working, they stayed with plan A.

And plan A was to hit us with direct, hard-running and attacking football. If that was good enough… great. If it wasn't, they'd come back the next day, tweak things ever so slightly… and go again.

Maughan was rewarded with a new three-year deal after steering us to the final in 2004. But he was gone within 12 months, after we lost again to Kerry in the 2005 quarter-final.

I was left out of the starting line-up for that game, after a poor match in the qualifier victory over Cavan. I failed to score and when Maughan announced the team to play Kerry, in the hotel before we left for Croke Park, I wasn't in it. It annoyed me at the time but I was pleased that Austin O'Malley held his place. He'd scored 0-3 against Cavan and was superb against Kerry, roasting Marc Ó Sé and taking five points from play.

I came on for Aidan Kilcoyne with 14 minutes of normal time left but we lost by three points. It was a blow that brought back memories of when I was left out of the team in 2002 but I knew that if I worked hard, like I did back then, that I'd get back in. Unfortunately, I didn't get the chance to work with John Maughan again.

But John Maughan and myself have stayed in touch ever since and when I was considering leaving the Mayo panel in 2012, he told me more than once to hang tough and stick it out. He mentioned on radio around that time that I'd scored seven points in a trial game, at a time when I was trying to force my way back into the team.

I called to correct him.

'I scored 10 points… not seven!' I announced.

Maughan only laughed.

'You're some boy!'

It was the lift that I needed at the time… but that was Maughan. I always knew that he had my back.

And he was the kind of manager that wouldn't expect you to do anything that he wouldn't do. If boys were struggling in runs, he'd step in.

'I'll do it,' he'd announce.

And invariably he would. It's difficult for me to understand the level of resentment that exists in Mayo towards him in certain quarters because I've always respected John Maughan.

Always have… always will. He wasn't everyone's cup of tea but as I've learned only too well for myself… who is?

CHAPTER 5

When I was finished, there was just one face staring back at me from the wall.

Don't ask me why but on the night I won my one and only All-Ireland medal, a Sigerson Cup with Dublin City University in 2006, I decided to rip a team photo to pieces.

I was left on my own in an apartment back on campus, where we had partied hard after DCU beat Queen's in February to win that Sigerson Cup… the Holy Grail of Third-Level football.

The rest of the lads were heading for Copper Face Jacks in the city but I couldn't because I had an FBD League final for Mayo against Galway the next day in Tuam.

That hadn't stopped me enjoying DCU's win though and there was plenty of whiskey on board when I decided to tear the poster from the wall.

Just one face was left when my job was done, that of Dublin goalkeeper Stephen Cluxton, my current Parnells clubmate.

To this day, I still have no idea why I did that.

I blame the whiskey because I vomited later and placed a bin on top of the evidence.

My uncle Jimmy was asleep in one of the rooms nearby and he was with me the next morning for the long trip to Tuam.

It was a morning when I must have died a thousand deaths on the way back west.

Mickey Moran and John Morrison asked me if I had been out and, of course, the response was no.

'Not at all... not a bother on me lads.'

Luckily enough I started on the bench but I was on before half-time.

Kieran Fitzgerald hit me an awful elbow into the stomach on the same day. I could feel my insides churning.

We lost by five points and after leaving the dressing room, I headed for Monaghan to continue the Sigerson party with the DCU boys. Brendan Egan, the Sligo player, wasn't boozing and he drove my jeep back to Dublin to cap off one hell of a weekend. Good times but that's what life was like in DCU.

I went there originally because I had heard stories from guys about what life was like in college, and the craic they were having. I was working like a dog at home in Shrule with the quarry business, 9-6 every day, while my friends were out doing what young lads do. There were two sides to that coin. I had money then and some of my mates didn't. They had their few bob for college, fine... but I had a car, could afford to go abroad on holidays and was looking after myself.

But there were days, too, when I was sitting at home on the couch, wondering what life was all about. As a mature student, direct entry courses provided me with the opportunity to pursue third level education.

I had a pass in my Leaving Cert and that was good enough to get in. James Lohan from Shrule was in DCU and I enquired about the place. Declan Brennan, Niall Moyna and Mickey Whelan, who had learned that I was interested in going there, then approached me separately.

They rang me regularly during the summer of 2005, made me feel wanted and that's where I decided to go.

I was 23 years old when I returned to full-time study and I qualified on a sports scholarship.

That was down to the fact that I was playing county football for Mayo but I had put together a good portfolio and I needed that to get through a rigorous vetting process.

There was the usual hullaballoo about DCU grabbing players but the guys I knew went to college primarily to gain academic qualifications. We played football, of course, but that's a limited shelf life and if your only aim from college is to play in the Sigerson Cup, you'll hardly be qualified for the workplace.

It still took me a while to grasp that concept.

It was D2 nightclub on a Monday, Quinn's in Drumcondra on the Tuesday, Coppers on the Wednesday and Thursday, and home on the Friday. We lived the life and a year or more passed before I copped on to the fact that attending lectures was a pretty big deal.

If it came down to a percentage point one way or the other in exams and assignments, you'd get the benefit of the doubt if your attendance levels were good. After that, I never missed a lecture, even if I'd been out the night before and got home in the early hours of the morning.

I knocked around with the footballers in college and we had some top class players. Cluxton, Bernard Brogan, Paul Casey, Bryan Cullen, Declan Lally and Ross McConnell were there from Dublin. We had Cavan's Seanie Johnston and Owen Lennon from Monaghan.

Other top players went through during my time there. Kevin Reilly was also on our Sigerson Cup winning team and I lived with the Meath player, sharing accommodation on campus with Brogan, and Monaghan's Ciaran 'Nudie' Hughes.

Sligo's David Kelly would also play for DCU, as well as Michael Murphy, captain of Donegal's 2012 All-Ireland winning team.

The calibre of player going through the place was frightening but the facilities at DCU were top class. Ken Robinson, CEO of DCU Sports, provided gym access and it wasn't just GAA players working out there. Fionnuala Britton and the late Darren Sutherland would go on to become Olympians.

I lived with Darren for three months after being thrown out of my own apartment.

And I don't think that Darren was too impressed with my lifestyle, which was far removed from his as a boxer. He would go on to win a bronze medal at the 2008 Beijing Olympics and I really didn't comprehend the scale of this guy's ambitions.

If you're talking about a 24/7 athlete, Darren was it.

He left a note on the fridge for me one morning, asking me if I could please replace the ham that I had raided the night before. I'd obviously come in after a few pints and satisfied my munchies with Darren's ham.

But Darren knew exactly what food he had in that fridge and how much of it he was consuming. And if there was a ham thief on the loose, he wanted the goods replaced – Darren was a good guy and we shared a similar interest in sports science.

He was attempting to juggle his studies with his boxing career, completing a term, training for 6-8 weeks and then coming back again to college. We swapped notes occasionally and news of his untimely death in September 2009 really hit me.

I rang Declan Brennan, his adviser, straight away and it's just so unfortunate that Darren didn't feel that he could speak to someone about his issues. I met Darren's parents, Tony and Lynda, numerous times and I remember that Tony was invited to speak to the Mayo squad when John O'Mahony was manager.

Gerry Hussey, sport psychologist with the Irish Olympic boxing team, was also involved with Mayo and Tony spoke to us while we were on a training camp at Johnstown House.

Tony described the journey that Darren embarked on to get to where he did. It was a message that left a lasting impact on our players and when Darren passed away, it struck a nerve with sportspeople across many codes.

Darren managed to reach the top of his profession and he symbolised the quest for sporting excellence at DCU.

As college footballers, and amateur sportspeople, we reached our greatest height with Sigerson Cup success and that feeling was indescribable.

If I could bottle and sell it, I'd have made a fortune.

We beat UCC in a tough semi-final at DCU's sports grounds and I was caught on camera aiming two fingers at a few Cork boys who were barking at me as I lined up a free.

We got through by two points and Saturday was one of those surreal days… one I'll never forget.

Uncle Jimmy had come up from Tuam for a few pints, and we were in the city centre on the morning of the final, a Saturday. It was February 25, the day when riots broke out because of a unionist march down O'Connell Street.

We were eating breakfast in a café on Parnell Street and while the situation hadn't kicked off fully by then, there was still a really tense atmosphere in the air and debris on the streets. Jimmy and I were curious; there were cameras everywhere but I had to go and prepare for the final at Parnell Park.

I left Jimmy to his own devices and he wished me luck.

'See you at the match.'

An hour later, there was mayhem on the streets but Jimmy just sat there and watched it all, engrossed. All he was missing was popcorn and a coke! And he did make it to Parnell Park to watch me win my first national medal.

I kicked a couple of big scores near the end with my right boot and felt elated. I knew we were home before full-time but I still couldn't believe it when the final whistle went.

I sought out Mam and Dad in the crowd and shared the moment with them. We ate some grub after the match in the clubhouse at Parnell Park but I was conscious of the FBD final the next day, and my promise to Moran and Morrison that I'd make it to Tuam. We had a few beers to celebrate and somehow, I managed to find a bottle of whiskey for the bus journey back to DCU, where we had planned a massive party back at the residences.

I swigged from that bottle on the short bus hop back and it was a wild blowout back at base. Liam Moffatt, physio with the Mayo squad, was studying in DCU at the time and had a new laptop, which was smashed during the party. That was an unfortunate episode but it was a massive celebration. As a group, we should have won more than just that one Sigerson but we were marked men from then on.

Other colleges resented us but study became more important too and commitment to football wasn't what it could have been. DCU won two more

Sigerson titles after I left, in 2010 and 2012, and a host of fine players have been involved, like Murphy from Donegal, Mayo goalkeeper Rob Hennelly and Colm Begley of Laois, who is playing club football with Parnells.

I was delighted to join a select band of players who won Sigerson Cup medals and I wildly imagined what it would be like to win the big one… the All-Ireland, with Mayo. When I left DCU in 2009, I did so with a heavy heart. I couldn't have asked much more from the place, or the people I met there.

Sigerson Cup winner with an honours degree in Sports Science!

Not too bad for the kid who cried at night in boarding school and who grew to resent the educational system. To Niall, Mickey, Giles Warrington, Siobhan McArdle, Brian Carson, Catherine Woods and Paul O'Connor, my heartfelt thanks.

You helped to make me a better man, and a better footballer.

PART TWO
One Sunday

CHAPTER

Billy Joe

Saturday, September 16, 2006:

Billy Joe Padden was always a great man for the jellies. Wine gums were his speciality.

'Here... throw us over a jelly, Billy.'

Eating sweets on the night before an All-Ireland senior football final might be a practice frowned upon by dieticians and nutritionists now, but holed up in our hotel room we'll do anything to pass the time.

Surely sweets are okay!

They're not chocolate... and they're not crisps. Somebody, somewhere must have told us that they were relatively healthy before a game.

I drove up from Mayo earlier today, via Julianstown in Meath for an ice-bath. It's a habit I adopted before our quarter-final against Laois and the semi-final with Dublin. And it works for me. I always feel fresh and loose after an ice-bath. A tenner for 10 minutes.

Money well spent.

The rest of the Mayo travelling contingent had arrived up on the bus by the time I reached Bewley's Hotel near the airport, our pre-match base.

That is one of the things that I like about our manager, Mickey Moran, and his sidekick, coach John Morrison. They let you do things like that. You don't have to be on the bus if you can get to the hotel yourself.

I know what works for me and what doesn't. A bit like the pre-match meals. I don't like pasta, never have. So I never have to eat it before games.

But I do like sweets.

And Billy Joe is always a man who has them in plentiful supply. Billy Joe is my roommate for the night… a thinking footballer… and a thinking man's footballer in equal measure.

And I like Billy Joe. He's an intelligent chap and always has a good outlook on the game. He's forever thinking about patterns in matches, the ebbs and flows, what teams should be doing… what we should be doing. Formations and tactics… he loves that kind of stuff.

He'll make a good coach one day, I always think to myself.

And he is confident before this game. I think we all are particularly after we have beaten Dublin in the semi-final. We feel that if we can hold things tight against Kerry until the 50th minute, and still be in there with a shout with 10 or 15 minutes to go, that we can close the game out.

The nightmare scenario is a repeat of 2004, when the game was over by half-time. Be in the game by the 50th minute… and see what can happen from there!

That's all we want.

And we have players who can score… when we need to make a run for the finish line in the last 10 or 15 minutes.

Ger Brady.

Ronan McGarrity.

Ciaran McDonald.

Alan Dillon.

Kevin O'Neill.

Billy Joe.

And me.

We feel confident that if we can gain a decent amount of possession that we can do damage. And we are tight at the back, too! We've only conceded four goals all season in the Championship.

Four in our previous six matches… two of those against Dublin.

I know Billy Joe from his younger days but we are different personalities as footballers. Billy Joe is calm and collected in everything that he does. He speaks with intelligence and always says the right stuff.

Me? I'm more inclined to shoot from the hip.

Billy Joe would never have told a reporter that Mayo would not win an All-Ireland without him! Billy Joe never makes a comment that he regrets. Billy Joe isn't like that, whereas I come out with the first thing that comes into my head.

And Billy Joe plays the game in that methodical way.

He is solid, knows what he is good at and works hard to improve his strengths. He is never the fastest or the most skilful but he is very accurate… strong… and a superb kick-passer.

I sometimes feel that Mayo don't utilise him enough. He doesn't get enough ball to make things happen… Alan Dillon the same.

Billy Joe and "Dillo" are two of our half-forwards but everything goes through the mercurial talent that is Ciaran McDonald.

That's the way it's been all through 2006.

And that's the way it's going to be tomorrow in the All-Ireland final.

I know that.

Ciaran knows it.

Kerry know it.

It is not a pre-ordained game plan or anything like that. It is simply because McDonald is so good… arrowing pinpoint deliveries into the inside line with the outside of that gifted left boot. McDonald is so strong, fit and powerful that he invariably becomes the hub in every game.

But Billy Joe and Dillo can play too. Billy Joe rarely misses and he can shoot off both feet. He takes a few knocks along the way and isn't picked as much as he should be. I'm not sure what the reasons are for that? Perhaps people don't think that he is pacey enough.

He played a few games in the full-forward line but that wasn't his position.

He is a half-forward, working between the lines, getting on the ball and pinging it inside. McDonald can pass… but so can Billy Joe.

He puts it just where you want it.

He never seems weighed down by that famous surname either. The son of Willie Joe, the Mayo legend from the 80s, but Billy Joe travels his own path, as does his brother David, a goalkeeper from our underage days. Within the county itself, I've never heard the comparisons. After all, Billy Joe is a forward and Willie Joe was a midfielder. A bit like my brothers, Kenneth and Trevor… different players. You can't compare like with like.

Billy Joe, if anything, feels that we are not aggressive enough in the big games. And he feels that was one of our biggest failings in 2004. He feels we didn't learn enough from that. It should have been experienced gained but there has been little or no learning. There is always the chance that things can go against us again tomorrow, and the key then is how will we react?

Over the last two years, we've never really discussed 2004.

If the team is under intense pressure, a cute player might go down and hold his leg, stop the flow and break the opposition's momentum.

Moran and Morrison are more content to trust our strengths and our ability. In the last week before the final, it has been all about us, which is good. Teams can worry too much about the opposition.

It's a Catch 22 thing. Of course we realise how good Kerry are but Moran and Morrison have confidence in us and they feel that if we fulfil our roles, and execute the game plan, that we'll win the game. Generally, if you can get on top in seven or eight positions, you're well on the way to winning the game. The problem with Kerry is… if they're on top in even four or five positions, and those players are Paul Galvin, Colm Cooper, Kieran Donaghy, Darragh Ó Sé and Tomas Ó Sé… well… then we might be in trouble.

***

Of course we are aware of that but the night before the game is a time for positivity. It isn't an ideal situation, though, staying in a hotel packed with

Mayo supporters. I told Billy Joe that I'd pop out to the shop a little while ago, but I didn't get as far as reception. After exiting the lift, which stopped behind double doors looking out into the foyer, all that I could see was a throng of Mayo people.

I high-tailed it back up the lift again.

Different players are experiencing different emotions. I am always one for bouncing around from room to room. I'm knocking around with Dillo, Pat Harte, Peadar Gardiner and my brother, Trevor. The older boys have their own thing going on. I wouldn't call it a clique but in many teams there's a natural gravitation towards certain individuals. Some players are going for a rub from the physio… drinking tea… ringing home to check if everyone is okay for tickets.

And Billy Joe has sweets.

Billy Joe dozed off in the room after *Match of the Day*.

It's after 1.0 a.m. and I'm going to nod off myself soon. A good night's sleep before the game is great but it's probably more important two nights before. Sports science tells us that. A good eight or nine hours on the Friday night always does me fine.

Too deep a sleep the night before a game and I'll feel tired.

Oddly enough.

Text messages have been beeping through with regularity and I know thumbing through them can sometimes heighten my anxiety levels. But what should I do instead? It's impossible to spend six hours in a hotel thinking about one game. If you decide to black out the whole world and go into your shell, it's very difficult to climb out of it.

So I never opt to go in there.

I just try to keep things as normal as possible. I keep telling myself that. But this is no ordinary night. This is the night before an All-Ireland senior football final.

It's a phenomenal occasion, I know that… from the moment I step through the doors of the hotel to the moment I step off the field at Croke Park after the game. I'm thinking about what I'm going to do when I get my first ball…

and my second ball.

I'm running it over... and over... in my head so many times... and once or twice I see myself losing the first ball... I'm on the back-foot right from the start.

Better not to think too much.

Maybe.

I'm thinking again.

I'll get my first touch, the feel of the leather and I'll go from there. Get the ball into my hand... turn this way and that... and bang... over the bar.

Four elements instead of one.

But my marker might be two yards in front of me... and I may not get the ball at all. It's hard enough, I know, to get the ball in an All-Ireland final in the first place.

Okay... okay... let it go.

Sleep.

We had a team meeting earlier this evening. That is part of the normal routine. Arrive at the hotel... have dinner... then meet. The mood is good. Moran and Morrison have reminded of us how they want us to play.

The "nut" formation up top... three inside.

The "nut" is where the three inside forwards converge before splitting off in different directions. It's a tactic aimed at keeping the full-backs guessing and on their toes. When it's done well, they'll struggle to react quickly enough.

Moran and Morrison decided to leave the room then.

We were left in silence for what seemed like an eternity.

A minute.

Minute and a half... maybe.

David Brady piped up.

'We're on our own now!'

Everyone laughed.

It's not the funniest thing anyone has ever said in the Mayo football team... but anything to break the ice.

I slept okay… eventually.
Pillows are a pain though.
They are double pillows.
When I'm at home, I like a flat one.
But we're here now.
No going back.

CHAPTER 7

Mickey Moran

Shortly after Mickey Moran was appointed as the new Mayo senior manager in October 2005, I met him in Castlebar. John Morrison was there too, a colourful Armagh man with a hugely positive outlook.

I warmed to them instantly.

They were friendly guys and they liked how I played. They talked about my role in the team straight away, and how they'd watched me over the years.

It was good stuff to hear, and right from the start I felt wanted.

Mickey took a back seat, to an extent, with Morrison coaching the team. He was on the phone to me a lot, nailing down my role and emphasising his vision of how he wanted me to play.

It was a personal touch and it's amazing what that can do for the confidence of a player. You'll hear the typical stuff from some managers... how you're on a par with the rest of the forwards and yet you know that you're not. I don't sit down and think that I'm better than another forward in the squad but, when I have the boxes ticked, I do know that I have more work done than a guy I might be competing with for a spot on the team.

It has always been that individual work that has kept me a step ahead. You don't play well on the weekend by just training on Tuesday and Thursday nights, and doing your gym work on Mondays and Wednesdays. It doesn't work like that. It takes practice. I remember scoring five points against Fermanagh in the 2004 All-Ireland semi-final replay, for example.

Three of them from play... and it was literally ball in hand... turn... shoot. At county level, you only get that split second.

My point is that the more I work on my shooting, the more confident I am of putting in a good performance. You're not born a better player than anybody else but you can practice harder.

The hardest workers will go the top.

All year long with the two lads, confidence has been high.

I'd won a Sigerson Cup with Dublin City University. I looked forward to training every single night and Trevor Howley, who I had some real tough battles with, marked me in a training game and remarked that I was showing All Star form. Coming from Trevor, that was a huge compliment. I'd get the better of him one night... he'd turn the tables another.

But you always earn your scores off Howley.

Moran and Morrison have repeatedly spoken about attitude and execution on the field of play. Morrison has drilled home the "nut" and how to run it.

Other coaches will tell you to run five or six times, to get free from a defender into open space. Morrison, however, takes it a step further. He wants me to get the ball in a certain area, where the team can benefit most. And so when I make those runs, my second last cut has to be right... so that on my last cut, I am getting the ball... turning... and shooting with my left foot.

A small thing but it was entirely new to me. To Morrison, where you are on the pitch means everything.

It is part of the master plan.

Attitude refers to how I apply myself in training.

I never allow myself to get negative. That is the attitude... be positive all of the time. A lot of this is down to Morrison. He speaks a lot more than Mickey, who is quiet. But when Mickey speaks… players listen.

I want to do well for these guys. I really want to play for them. And that is important. But it's been that way with all the Mayo managers I've played for.

Psychologically, I improve with experience.

I can get down in myself if I am struggling in the first few minutes of games… if the ball isn't breaking for me. Morrison drives it into me … next ball.

Even in club football now, it's a big part of my make up. And I'll encourage my teammates if they make a mistake, instead of bawling them out of it, as I would have done once upon a time. Mind-set is hugely important in sport, I grew to learn. I wouldn't have thought that for years. I was sceptical of sport psychologists talking to me… lads who had never played the game, never experienced the pressure cooker environment.

How could he tell me how to handle a situation he's never been in himself? And I didn't believe that you can plan for the pressure of 80,000 people screaming at you. It's fine on a club pitch with nobody watching but in a packed Croke Park… it's a completely different thing.

Moran and Morrison helped me with tunnel vision on the job at hand. And Moran is true to his word. At that first meeting he'd spoken about what he wanted to achieve and how he was going to achieve it. He spoke about winning a Connacht Championship and an All-Ireland title. He believed that we had the potential to do it and instilled us with that belief.

I don't think we have over-achieved this year… reaching an All-Ireland final.

We have natural footballers, we were the dominant team in Connacht and so it was no surprise to many that we won the provincial title. I kicked the winner in the final against Galway in Castlebar… a difficult free from a tight angle… 13 metres out.

It was redemption for the one I'd missed on my debut in 2002.

Some of the same supporters who had hammered me four years previously were trying to lift me up onto their shoulders after the game.

I just ran into the dressing room.

***

There were other good moments this season, particularly against Laois in our two All-Ireland quarter-finals.

I scored six points in the drawn game, including another late free to ensure a replay. Five points in the replay, and another three frees… but the points from play gave me huge satisfaction because I was up against Joe Higgins, one of the finest corner backs in the country. Higgins has pace to burn but I managed to come out on top against him.

And that pleased me because as a corner forward, you must judge yourself against the finest corner backs. I got five more points against Dublin, three from play this time, in a classic semi-final that was settled by a late wonder score by Ciaran McDonald. Confidence was high.

Moran and Morrison helped to see to that.

The training drills helped to benefit forwards – plenty of diagonal ball and good use of the "nut". It is all to benefit us as a team, with hard work and footballing intelligence underpinning everything that we do.

What we have planned for Kerry is sound in theory, but will prove far more difficult to execute in practice.

But yeah, we're confident.

And why wouldn't we be?

We are Mayo.

Grandad George

Sunday, September 17, 2006:

THE morning light brings with it a stark realisation.

This is All-Ireland final Sunday.

No hiding place.

A morning like no other.

It's a day when dreams can be shattered or it could be the day when an All-Ireland Senior Football Championship famine dating back to 1951 finally comes to an end. For a county with such a proud footballing tradition as Mayo's, that's far too long. The morning newspapers will tell us that, but I tend to steer clear of them on match days.

I had a scan through them yesterday alright.

More time killed.

It was strange reading them. Interviews conducted a couple of weeks before from the press night are brought back to life on the pages the day before the big game.

My late grandfather, George is foremost in my mind. It's just a few days since he was buried and that was a tough… tough day. George was my world to a large degree growing up, driving me to school and matches, and to the Mayo School of Excellence when I was in my early teens.

He passed away on the Saturday evening, shortly after I returned home from training. I knew he was sick but I didn't let myself believe that it was that bad. My father told me to call in to see George before I went to training.

And I rang Trevor, who was living in Tuam, and urged him to pop in too. It was as if Dad knew… a sixth sense. George was sleeping in bed.

That's what I told myself, he's just sleeping. And I was bothered at training. We were playing a silent game, where nobody speaks. It's a deliberate thing, preparation for Croke Park where you won't hear yourself think… never mind your teammates roaring for a pass.

You don't talk… you just see.

And the good teams in Croke Park can do that. They see a pass, as opposed to hearing it. The more well oiled the machine, the better.

It works on instinct. What Moran and Morrison want is for us not to hit a man with a pass specifically, but to hit an area. At training, we have a big square outside what is now the "D".

We run from the halfway line to the 45 metre line and then kick the ball into the square. That's all the player sending in the ball is asked to do. Then it is up to the forward to do what he has to do to get free and collect possession. Space is the key but it requires hard work from the inside forwards.

There's plenty of space on a football pitch, no matter how tight marking the opposition is, but clever movement is required to create and exploit it. And the real secret for a forward is to make that space valuable to you.

That sounds pretty simplistic but how many times in a game have we all seen one inside forward running in the same direction as another, with the third guy holding the middle?

That's why the "nut" has worked so well for us, because we have three forwards breaking off in different directions. Of course, good defenders will cop on to this after a while and, if they're clever, all it takes is a jersey pull to stop the forward breaking quickly. But at the same time, it is new to us and it has worked against opponents so far.

We have worked hard at it… night after night. Three of us together and…

then... 'NNNUUUTTTTT!'

Split.

It might only work once in a game but if the "nut" brings us a score, it could win the game for us by a point.

Another tactic of ours is to ask our two corner forwards to sprint out to midfield as hard as they can for the throw-in.

We bank on winning possession straight away and hitting the one guy left inside on the edge of the square. It's a move aimed at trying to score an early goal. I'm not a prolific goal-scorer, unfortunately.

And my record of 14 goals in 99 League and Championship appearances for Mayo is a source of disappointment to me.

There are times when I try to take the net out of it, instead of going low... and the ball flies over the bar. As players become more experienced, they roll the ball into the corner or try to dummy the goalkeeper before tapping it in. But I have been a top corner or nothing man for too long.

Goals are hard to come by but some forwards make it look so easy now... far easier than I find it. Bernard Brogan from Dublin is a clinical finisher... Colm Cooper in Kerry... Cork's Colm O'Neill, and our own Cillian O'Connor, who is so cool in front of goal.

Good forwards like that are clinical almost all of the time, whether it's in the heat of an inter-county game playing in front of 82,000 people at Croke Park or in the local grounds with their clubs. Their appreciation of space and their ability to get free from tight marking defenders marks them out and separates them from the rest. And they're the ones who make the silent games look easy.

At that training session last Saturday night, it was not working out for me. I was distracted. George was on my mind.

Ger Brady didn't hit me with two passes and I bawled him out of it. Moran and Morrison asked me what was wrong ?

I shrugged my shoulders, and headed for home.

My 'phone was red with texts and missed 'phone calls.

My sister, Tara was urging me to get home as quickly as I could. When I arrived back to George's place, the family was gathered around his bed.

It was time.

The priest had been there to administer the Last Rites.

We could only wait now.

We were waiting on Dermot to arrive from Kildare.

He made it around five o'clock.

And that was it.

When Dermot walked into the room, George took his last breath. I had my arm held gently under his neck when he passed away.

My uncle Stan told me that George was gone.

It was all so final.

Trevor and I can now honour his memory in the best possible fashion, by bringing home the Sam Maguire Cup.

But not having him there will be strange. He was so proud of us all and the fact that Kenneth, Trevor and I wore the green and red puffed out his chest no end. While we were training as kids, he'd sit in the car and read the newspaper. When we were finished, he'd drive us home again. He managed to drag himself up out of bed to watch the Dublin game and he'd have done the same for Kerry too. But the sands of time have run out for George.

A light went out in my world. It was so hard and difficult, but the fact that we were playing football and preparing for an All-Ireland final helped me to cope.

Life goes on.

That's what everyone says eventually.

You don't forget but you get so caught up in every other bit of s*** that's going on in your life, and you try not to think about it.

Grief is a funny thing. It depends on how you control it, I think. You could sit there wailing for weeks, but I tried to block it out and move on. I had to. People might not think that this is a great way to handle things but when you lose someone, you have to move on.

What's the alternative?

I have tried not to dwell on George's death but his memory lives on. Any time we are down in Granny's house we talk about him. I call to the grave now and then, to say hello.

Like a lot of things, it's something I will be doing more of – but, at the same time, I realise that if you did everything that you wanted and needed to do, there would be no time for anything else.

I rang Mam and Dad to see where they are?

I asked them did they know where they're going, and suggested a good place to park their car. I'll only be happy when they're in the stadium… it's out of my control then.

I always worry about the ticket situation.

They'll have to meet people to get sorted and I can't be on the 'phone to help sort that out. I can only control what I can control.

We find ourselves queuing up for breakfast with Mayo supporters.

Not great.

Don't get me wrong… we weren't hassled or anything like that… and they mean well. But it's very difficult to have a conversation with somebody that you don't know on the morning of an All-Ireland final.

'How are you getting on?' they ask.

'Grand.'

'Looking forward to the match?' they ask again.

'Yeah.'

That is the time to get some food in… say a silent prayer… walk around… be quiet… don't expend any energy.

Managers have told us in the past that if we are walking down the street and somebody approaches, pretend to be on the mobile phone.

No distractions.

Even talking is losing energy and, on this morning of all mornings, we'll use energy without even knowing it.

But this is poor planning.

Supporters have our best interests at heart but it's not the time to be mingling with them.

***

After breakfast I'm back to the room and my bag is packed.

Tracksuit... boots...

Gloves... wash bag... towel.

I have another bag with me, with clothes for the next couple of days. Just in case. My boots are hard and crisp. I left them on the radiator last night.

They'll feel tighter on my feet, and that will make for a better ping off the ball when I kick it. Not an ideal situation having the heat on in the room at full blast to dry out my boots but it was another box ticked.

Normally, at home, I'd have my boots in the boiler room.

The text messages are still flying.

Well-wishers.

Walking through the hotel it's difficult to switch off.

Hustle and bustle.

More good wishes.

We're not engaging and that is coming across as rude. But it's not intentional. Win an All-Ireland and I'll talk to these people for the rest of my life.

Not just now.

If they think I'm being rude... fine.

I'm acknowledging them but words are in short supply. Some guys have not even come down from their rooms yet... and it's almost time to board the coach.

But I'm feeling giddy.

The itinerary was straightforward.

Breakfast... bus... Croke Park... and do what you can in between to pass the other minutes.

Nerves are building.

My stomach churning.

I'll do it for George.

CHAPTER 9

Austin O'Malley

All-Ireland finals can spawn the most unlikely of heroes.

In the local and national press, the build-up has been dominated by talk of who might step up to the plate and take the game by the scruff of the neck?

"Have Mayo learned from 2004 or will Kerry rule again?"

The main protagonists are the chosen ones…. the guys who chatted to the media at the press nights… saying plenty but revealing little.

The teams had been picked and journalists were left to speculate on the match-ups. "Surely Tom O'Sullivan will pick up Mortimer again…

"… he did such a good job on him two years ago."

Speculation… speculation.

For the guys not involved, it can be a difficult time. They remain supportive but inside… they're dying. Austin O'Malley is one of these men.

A man whose county career is passing him by.

I wouldn't have known a lot about Austy when he joined the Mayo senior panel a couple of years ago. He was playing for Louisburgh and racking up big scores at club level on a consistent basis.

And when he got on the training field, it was easy to see why he was making a name for himself. He could have been cut from granite. But all year long Austy seems to be the fall guy. He was subbed in almost all of our League games, started against London in the first round of the Championship but didn't score... and got dropped for the victory over Leitrim.

From then on, Austy was on the outside looking in.

But I think that we could be doing more with him. He looks after himself terrifically well, and is very strong and accurate with both feet. He impressed me right from the start, ticked all the boxes.

He still looks after himself, watches what he eats, does his weights. The six-pack is still there and he's still playing brilliantly with Louisburgh. I always admire Austy's attention to detail and I often wonder why his Mayo career hasn't work out the way he would have wanted.

Successive Mayo managers perhaps looked at Austy and formed an incorrect impression that he is mentally weak. Austy is quiet and doesn't say a whole lot and maybe that creates the impression that he is nervous. There are games that Mayo have played and I couldn't understand why he wasn't involved. He might have marked Keith Higgins in a training match and kicked points for fun but, when Sunday came, he didn't get his chance.

I've grown close to Austy over the years.

I'd head out in Westport with him, have some dinner, drink a couple of beers and we practice together too. I can feel his pain when he isn't playing. He'll be p***** off and ring me, searching for answers.

But I can't help him much.

It isn't my place to go ringing the manager.

But I've learned loads from Austy, particularly in terms of what you should be doing away from the training field. One thing I don't do enough of is stretching but Austy is devoted to it. He has different mats... works on the foam roller, and is at the physio quite often for a massage. But still Austy has terrible problems with his hamstrings.

He'll look after some injury or other and will never go back to training until it is one hundred per cent right.

Ninty-nine per cent isn't enough.

He knows his body better than anyone that I know, studies things online, looks at the latest fitness fads and workouts. He'd see a guy using an exercise band and wonder what that was for?

Two days later, Austy has one.

He'll do anything to be on top of his game and better than the next man. But he rarely gets the chance to show what he can do.

And yet he remains positive, speaks passionately at team meetings and helps to keep spirits up at difficult times. As a Championship footballer, Austy just needs that run, the confidence to know that even if things don't work out for him, he'll be there on the field again the next day.

We have plenty of good footballers but not many that are as effective as Austy with both feet. He could be a vital cog today… a game-changer.

And, by God, against Kerry that might be something wonderful.

CHAPTER 10

Alan Dillon

IT'S all becoming very real now.

Bags packed.

Time to get on the bus… time to gather my thoughts.

The bus is parked in a quiet bay but we still have to make our way through a swathe of Mayo fans. Well-wishers, as I say… but I'd still prefer things a little bit quieter… a whole lot quieter

You might think there's plenty of chat on our bus as we make our way to Croke Park for an All-Ireland final, but there isn't. For other games, sure, but not this time.

It's too big.

The nerves are too great.

And they're kicking in now.

Big time.

Ear-phones on… and away.

I tried to find a window seat near the back… failed… and grabbed a seat up the front.

***

I used to sit beside Dillo a lot.

Like me, he hasn't been one for the music until later years. Andy Moran is bouncing around, all energy.

I'm reinforcing again.

The boxes are ticked

I tell myself that.

Ticked.

Ticked.

Ticked.

I keep reminding myself of every little box.

Trust in my ability.

Everything will fall into place now.

Preparation is done.

Just go out and bring what I've prepared for.

Theoretically, there is no need to be nervous but it's impossible not to be. And I'm a firm believer that the nerves have to be there… to get a performance. The body knows that something big is coming. There would be something wrong if I wasn't nervous now.

For club and county, it's always been that way. I wouldn't have liked it said that I didn't play well in a game for the club. It's important to me to play as well as I can in every single game.

It's a Catch 22 thing though.

The more I think about the game, the more nervous I become.

So I try to tune into my music.

Our normal route for Croke Park.

We go past The Big Tree pub in Drumcondra… and that's when the heart skips a beat. I peer out through the glass, looking for a friendly face… or someone I know. The Mayo people are waving and cheering, hope in their hearts and joy on their faces. Believers.

Dreamers.

Realists.

I wonder what it would be like to help win an All-Ireland for these people. They'll be roaring us home, God willing, but right now they're enjoying the beer and the atmosphere.

A part of me wants to be out there with them, that desire to run away again, but... there's no hiding place. The All-Ireland final is a day like no other.

Connacht finals... All-Ireland quarter-finals and semi-finals... they don't compare. The footpaths are packed and as I'd suspected, the chances of seeing someone that I know are slim to none.

They're like giant ants.

Green and gold... red and green.

We're a couple of hours from throw in and there are no words that can adequately express the sheer rush that is the bus ride to Croke Park.

The stadium's skyline comes into view.

Another big moment.

Another heartbeat skipped.

Nerves rising... even higher.

Stomach churning... furiously.

On other days, travelling away from home for Championship games or League matches, the music in my ears really does something.

Toe-tapping... humming along.

Not this time.

I'm focused on my role and what I can do.

Keep it simple... keep it simple.

The work is done.

I've practiced and practiced.

Maybe I've overdone it. But I reckon the more practice I've put in, the easier it will be. I've kicked pressure frees because I've practiced.

Putting them over the bar in an All-Ireland final will be different.... I know that... try not to think about that.

A 14-yard free at Croke Park is not a technically difficult skill but the surroundings and the situation are different. It's okay when nobody's watching… 82,000 pairs of eyes is a different story.

Alan Dillon and I are as thick as thieves.

I first met him when we were kids attending the Mayo School of Excellence. He was a vocational schools player then, with Davitt College. In 2000 they lost an All-Ireland final replay against Coláiste Na Sceilge from Caherciveen in Kerry. Jack O'Connor was the Coláiste Na Sceilge manager and Declan O'Sullivan scored two points.

Two Dromid Pearses men…

… and we'll face them both at Croke Park today.

Alan progressed through the ranks and we played minor and Under-21 together for Mayo. We were also on a Connacht interprovincial underage team and I was picked for Ireland, along with Brian Naughton from Tourmakeady, a hell of a player in his day but a player who suffered terribly with injuries.

I went into the Mayo senior panel a year before Dillo did. Pat Holmes had asked him in but he didn't want to go in a year too early. He was playing quite a lot of football in other grades and competitions at the time.

I remember Dillo playing some football at corner forward when he was younger, at full-forward too. Dillo and his brother, Gary would rotate between centre-forward and full-forward but Dillo was never really an inside player. He's better facing goal than with his back to goal. When he first arrived on the scene, we were living the dream, playing for Mayo, wearing the red and green. He cut his teeth in the FBD League, the secondary provincial competition, and it wasn't long before our friendship blossomed.

We became the proverbial peas in a pod.

Dillo's a lot like me.

Serious about his football when he has to be, but laid back at other times, and well able to have the craic and the banter. There were plenty of Saturday nights when we'd head into the cinema in Castlebar.

I'd order the box of sweets, popcorn and Coke.

Dillo would stay on the water.

He was good like that, particular about his diet. He's the man I'd credit with introducing me to salads, when we travelled abroad together a few years ago.

He's a clever boy too, is Dillo.

Bottom line is that Dillo's highly-educated and qualified, an intelligent fella and good with money. He won't waste it.

He's a good trainer too and while he has struggled with injuries, Dillo comes back for more each season. He's very dedicated and playing for Mayo is a major part of his life. It's all he's known, to an extent, living and working in Mayo.

I sometimes wonder if I'd stuck around... if I was at home all of the time? But living in Dublin made it difficult for me. For Dillo there was none of the travelling that became the norm in Dublin for me.

Three hours in the car to Mayo... train... three hours back.

It takes its toll. Anybody who drives for three hours to training shouldn't train. Sports science will tell you that.

It's madness, really.

Towards the end of 2009, we decided to get away for a tour of Australia, New Zealand and South Africa... 13 weeks.

The life of Reilly.

Bungee jumps... sky dives... sight-seeing... and training.

We'd try to get in two or three sessions a week, on local parks, but the cabin fever set in towards the end. Dillo was at one end of the pitch and I was at the other... going through our drills.

It was only natural, I guess.

No matter how close you are to someone, or how much you like him or her, there comes a time when you need your space. But I always know that Dillo's there when I need him.

We'd have bitched about this and that when we were younger. Clutching at straws really, after a defeat. Searching for answers in the wrong places. Talking over dinner about who played s***, and downing a couple of beers.

Dillo's ready for this.

He was awesome against Dublin in the semi-final, but the All-Ireland final two years ago never worked out for him. Football's like that.

You play well on some days but on others, it doesn't work out. Still, if you can emerge from your career with more good days than bad, you've had a good one.

Like me, Dillo's a fan of Morrison and Moran.

He is another player they have placed their trust in. So much of our play goes through McDonald, perhaps to Alan's detriment, but Dillo still has had a good year and could win an All Star for himself. Me too… I could win an All Star.

Me and Dillo on the stage together… All Stars?

Imagine that.

He chipped in with points from play and took some serious scores against Dublin in the semi-final. And it was pretty difficult for a wing-forward to get on the score-sheet on such a regular basis. We were bypassing the half-forward line quite a lot with long direct ball and Dillo's involvement in games depends to a large extent on what McDonald is doing.

If McDonald is involved heavily, you will not see as much of Dillo. And the opposite also applies.

Dillo's quiet on the bus but he always goes quiet before games. He's on the earphones too, presumably listening to what I'd consider to be depressing music. Stuff like Evanescence.

Slow, methodical music.

Thinking man's music.

It works for him.

Me?

I've got Eminem to Tiësto… Keane to Coldplay.

But whatever I'm listening to now, it's not registering.

CHAPTER 11

James Nallen

THE team bus takes us deep into the bowels of Croke Park, on the Hogan Stand side of the field. We disembark… and immediately a TV camera crew is waiting for us.

Faces are tense.

There's a security guy outside of our dressing room door… a familiar face I've seen a few times before.

Some brief banter helps to break the ice.

Once inside the dressing room, the world closes in again.

Nowhere to hide.

I drop the bags and walk around for a bit, until I'm almost boring a hole in the floor. There are doubts surfacing.

I feel like I don't want to leave here.

The nerves are at their worst now, all consuming… almost.

What's it going to be like… out there?

I decide to find out… the minor final between Roscommon and Kerry is on.

It's a nice afternoon… fresh.

I watch the minor game for 10 minutes.

Soak in the whole day.

I return to my spot in the dressing room… close to a sink and with plenty of space around me.

Everyone suddenly dives for the match programmes that have been left on a table in the centre of the dressing room. Another icebreaker…

Whose face will adorn the front cover?

Turns out, there are four… I'm one of them.

Our goalkeeper David Clarke is also there… along with Kerry's Diarmuid Murphy and Kieran Donaghy.

Everything's laid out for us by our kit man, Liam Ludden.

A good man to bum the occasional cigarette from… I always found. Not that I was ever a regular smoker.

Just the odd one… here and there.

I could do with one now.

The fridges are stacked with Powerade and the bottles are freezing, just how they should be. Still no chat… high fives aplenty.

The subs are brilliant, wishing us luck as the enormity of what's ahead of us closes in. And there's Ludden, quietly going about his business.

He always has a big job to do, getting the bibs ready… the gear… water… cones and nets. He's always at training an hour before everybody else and leaves an hour after us all.

And he's doing all of this for us.

He was always so particular about the gear. We were entitled to a certain amount each year but I was always on the hunt for more.

Kenneth always told me that you can never have enough because when your career ends, you'll be left with none of it. I remember a night in Castlebar when Ludden had the door to the room where the kit was housed left open. Normally that door was always locked but Ludden let his guard down, and I managed to nab a couple of extra pairs of short and t-shirts.

To this day, I have a t-shirt at home belonging to Peadar Gardiner, and one of Trevor's pairs of shorts. But through the years I found that gear always went just as Kenneth had warned me. You'd give stuff to kids after games and people are on from different charities all the time looking for donations.

There's no way that you can turn them down.

Moran and Morrison are pacing the room, reassuring the players... giving us a gee-up.

'Alright boy?'

'Ready to go?'

I decide to head into the warm-up room next door.

No need to tog out just yet.

Tracksuit will do fine for now.

Some guys are getting rubs from the physio, others are taping up. Some still have the earphones in.

The warm-up room is pretty intense.

There's not a huge amount of space so we keep it simple.

Hand passing, kick passing... stretching.

No real hitting yet. Passing... passing... and if a ball gets dropped, the guilty party gets f***** out of it.

And that's fine.

It's important to be focused.

I'm not a big fan of warm-ups. I'd rather be out on the pitch having a few kicks at goal but, All-Ireland final day is all about protocol. It's not our time yet... won't be for a while.

The clock is ticking. Endlessly, it seems.

***

We need James Nallen today more than ever.

It's his fourth time around the block, fifth if you factor in the 1996 All-Ireland final replay. And Jimmy's a legendary character in Mayo, having won an All-Ireland club medal with Crossmolina in 2001. I've watched Jimmy playing since I was a young boy, as he was one of Kenneth's Mayo teammates.

Into an amateur world Jimmy has brought a huge degree of professionalism. He's a quiet guy but when he speaks, he speaks sense. He isn't one of those players who speaks just for the sake of it. Whenever Jimmy decides to say a few words, there is always true meaning in his message. He says what he says for a reason.

He also scored one of the most iconic goals in Mayo history – a spectacular effort against Kerry in the 1996 All-Ireland semi-final. But kicking was never really Jimmy's strongest point. I could be standing at the door and he wouldn't kick it straight to me. Though Jimmy is a brilliant centre back.

In Mayo there is simply no one better.

We are not the best of friends, Jimmy and I.

He is a lot older than me, for a start, and he has his own circle.

Jimmy hails from a good family and his brother Tom, known as "The Riddler", was also a cracking defender in his day. I often mark Jimmy in training and he is an exceptional worker. He is one of the squad's most dominant characters, not so much because of how he speaks.

It is more the aura that Jimmy has.

He is respected not only in Mayo, but also right across Ireland. Jimmy isn't the biggest fella in the world but he is strong, wiry and pacey. He's also a fitness freak. Jimmy has an engine that few can match and that allows him to play the centre back role well, getting up the pitch to support attacks while also drifting behind the half-back line to provide extra cover to the full-backs.

When I first joined the Mayo senior squad, I was almost afraid to speak to him. But he was one of the guys who welcomed me in with open arms and it is always nice to hear a 'hard luck' or a 'well done' from Jimmy. It means so much coming from him.

He is always excellent in the dressing room and a real motivator. Jimmy always has the last word or the second last word before we leave the room and it is never a shout or a roar.

'Play hard... do what we're supposed to do...' he'll say.

'... and we'll win this!'

Simple, effective language. And when the chips are down, you can always count on Jimmy to step up with a big tackle or a big play.

In all this time, I never have had a run in with Jimmy, and I played against him on numerous occasions. He is not a dirty footballer... he beats you with pure football and athleticism rather than resorting to the dark arts.

And at club level, he is a player I might get a score or two off if I'm marking him, whereas I'd feel confident of five or six against another defender. Whenever Jimmy loses a game, he hurts badly.

His body language and facial expression gives it away.

You see it in his eyes. But now those eyes are fiery, alive. He knows, like the rest of us, just how big a chance this is. He's carried the pain of 1996, 1997 and 2004 and finally getting his hands on a coveted All-Ireland medal would mean the world to him. He has climbed the mountain of regret and now finds himself on the cusp of greatness again.

And Jimmy knows that this could be his last chance.

They don't keep coming around. He knows 1996 was the one that got away and while Mayo had a better team than Kerry in '97, Maurice Fitzgerald just turned it on. So this has to be it.

Jimmy Nallen knows that.

CHAPTER 12

John Morrison

THE fear is back.

I don't think I can go out there.

Nerves have reached fever pitch. We're minutes before we leave the safety… sanctity almost… of this dressing room and face the light.

I don't like this time. Ten minutes… and out of here.

It's coming close. I'd rather be out there.

But… we've been here before. I've heard the sounds, smelled the smells. Studs are tapping furiously on the dressing room floor.

If I go into the toilets I'm sure I'll find someone vomiting into one of the toilet bowls.

Time to go to war.

Go over the top.

Again.

I know what that's like.

How terrifying it's going to be for a little while.

But… it's as it must be.

It's our job.

Today… this Sunday… this is my whole life.

***

I'm nervous beyond nervous.

Others are quiet.

We need our strong characters now.

David Brady... Jimmy.

We get into a huddle.

Brady... Nallen... and David Heaney are speaking.

It's from the heart.

'We owe these!'

I don't speak... never have before games.

It's hard enough trying to concentrate on what I have to do.

And the last thing I want is to talk in a dressing room and then go out... and play s***. That's just setting myself up for a fall. Some guys can manage that. Talk before the game, play s*** and yet it doesn't seem to affect them.

But it would affect me.

It would kill me.

I keep telling myself that I deserve to be here... that I can play.

I need to win the first ball and go from there.

Lose it, and I'll need to be very strong mentally to go again for the second one. Because the nerves will only get worse and the confidence will drain. I've been to the toilet to unload.

Maybe it's just a psychological thing but taking a dump before a game will make me feel more light-footed. A lot of players go because they're so nervous, not necessarily because they have to. We're two hours after the pre-match meal.

Better to go now... and be free... to run.

This is a unique occasion but I'm furiously telling myself that it's just another game. I take my mind to the dressing room in Shrule.

Keep it simple.

Think too much about this and I'm finished before I even start.

We're confident and rightly so.

But it's been another season of peaks and troughs. It reminds me of 2004, when we played the then champions Tyrone in the quarter-final. We knocked them out but struggled past Fermanagh over the course of two semi-finals... drawn match and replay. If we had beaten Fermanagh well, maybe we would have bounced into the final in a better frame of mind. But, God only knows how the subconscious works? In this campaign, we've come through a tough Connacht final before getting past Laois in the All-Ireland quarter-finals, where that second game was required. And then we beat Dublin in a classic.

Up and down again.

Are we stronger, more confident than 2004?

Difficult to say.

Everything is a blur. Comparisons are impossible. Do the job... keep it simple... first ball... turn... and bang.

It's all about ticking the boxes.

I can't fault our preparations but Austin O'Malley reckons that we made one error in the build-up.

And I can't argue.

At the media night, fans were on the pitch, watching us training, taking pictures of us at close quarters. As players, we didn't get anything out of that training session. It was a complete waste of time but in the greater scheme of things, it's a minor detail right now.

But it's made me realise just how important it is to prepare in minute detail. I can understand why counties go into lock down and ban supporters from attending training sessions. That might inconvenience people but, to have no excuses, you don't want anyone knowing what you're doing behind closed doors. The only people who should really know what's going on are players and management.

That's the hard thing about the relationship with fans. You can't fully shut them out but sometimes you have to, because I found it difficult not to get caught up in the hype again. Even yesterday, I was getting calls and text

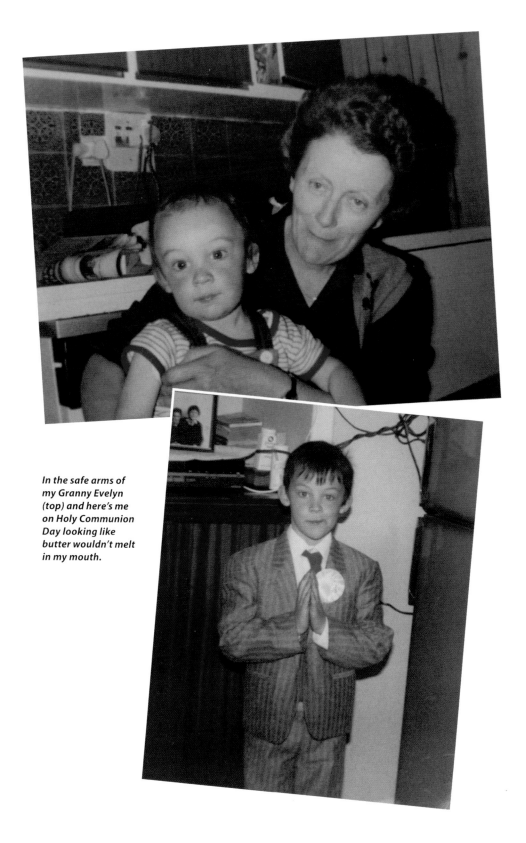

In the safe arms of my Granny Evelyn (top) and here's me on Holy Communion Day looking like butter wouldn't melt in my mouth.

Me, Trevor and Tara at primary school in Shrule.

My parents, Frank and Carmel on the day of my graduation from the University of Ulster, Jordanstown with a Masters in Sports and Business Management.

Grandad George, my father Frank, Tara, me, my mother Carmel and Trevor before I jetted off to Australia to represent Ireland in the Under-17 Compromise Rules Internationals in 1999.

Kevin Walsh, Dermot Geraghty, me, and Ronan Walsh getting a really good send-off from Shrule before the 2000 All-Ireland minor football final against Cork (top); and celebrating victory for Shrule-Glencorrib after the 2005 county senior football Championship semi-final against Charlestown with Granddad George, Kenneth's wife Glenda, my godchild Jenna and Kenneth.

My fiancée Sara and I celebrate our engagement.

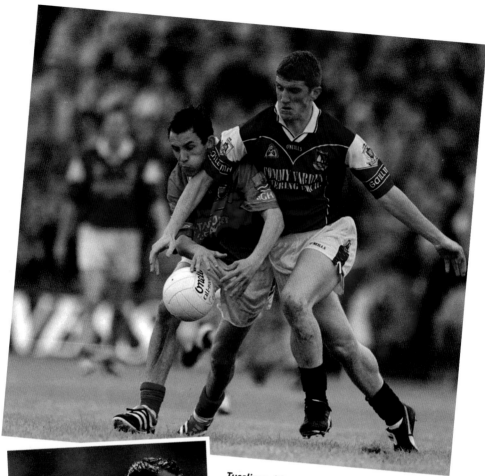

Tussling with Kieran Fitzgerald on my Championship debut for Mayo against Galway in Castlebar in 2002.

My early minor (above) and senior appearances for Mayo were strictly jet black hair days.

On the move against Fermanagh in the All-Ireland semi-final in 2004, with Ciaran McDonald willing me on (top); and we line up before the 2004 All-Ireland final against Kerry.

Our captain David Heaney leads us out onto the field, and past the Sam Maguire Cup, before the 2006 All-Ireland final against Kerry.

The Mayo and Kerry teams parade before the 2006 final.

Mickey Moran (left) and John Morrison who did a great job in leading us to the All-Ireland final in 2006.

Alan Dillon gets by Marc Ó Sé in the early stages of the 2006 final.

Ciaran McDonald finds himself caged in by the Kerry defence in the 2006 All-Ireland final.

Trevor looks to find a man in the 2006 final (top); and Ronan McGarrity gets to grips with Kerry midfielder Darragh Ó Sé.

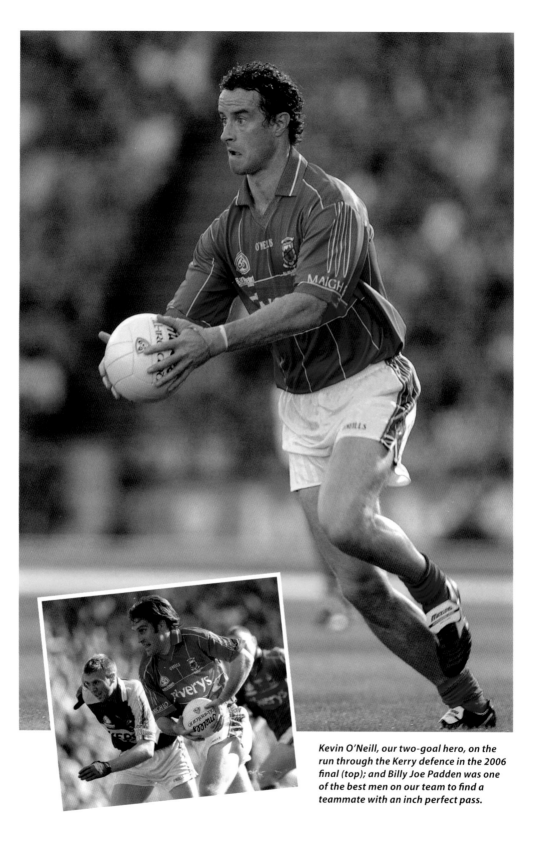

Kevin O'Neill, our two-goal hero, on the run through the Kerry defence in the 2006 final (top); and Billy Joe Padden was one of the best men on our team to find a teammate with an inch perfect pass.

Tom O'Sullivan shows why he is one of Kerry's best defenders as he breaks the ball away from me in the 2006 final (top), and later I win the ball and look for a way by him.

Kieran Donaghy and Colm Cooper celebrate a Kerry goal in the 2006 final, and Donaghy whips up the Kerry supporters.

The industry of Paul Galvin on the day was unbelievable as always.

David Brady (left) and Declan O'Sullivan have to be torn apart during the latter stages of the game.

David Brady consoles me after the game (top); and Tomás Ó Sé has a word and a hug for Ciaran McDonald.

The loneliness of Croke Park once the final whistle goes is shattering, as I take in the magnitude of the 2006 All-Ireland final defeat (top) and Peadar Gardiner troops back to our dressing room.

Kerry's Declan O'Sullivan and Colm Cooper lift the Sam Maguire Cup.

I celebrate a score for DCU in our Sigerson Cup victory in February 2006.

I shoot against Galway despite the attention of Damien Burke in the Connacht final in Castlebar in 2008.

After scoring my goal against Galway in the 2009 Connacht final in Salthill I decided to pay my own personal tribute to the late Michael Jackson... which did not impress many people outside the Jackson family.

I'm on the run against Dublin in Castlebar in the National League in 2012, the day I became Mayo's top scorer of all time.

I receive my All Star award at the end of the 2006 season from GAA President, Nicky Brennan and myself and Alan Dillon with our 2006 All Star awards.

messages from people looking for tickets.

That's the All-Ireland football final.

Nature of the beast. And now it's here.

Austin O'Malley reminded me of one of the great John Morrison stories. The day before the Connacht final victory over Galway, Morrison addressed the group at a team meeting. He brought up a story about one of his friends in the north, a guy by the name of John Smith. This guy John was taken by some guys, blindfolded and brought on a helicopter ride.

While in the air, the helicopter door was opened and Smith was pushed out. But the 'chopper was just three feet off the ground... and Smith had a soft landing. Morrison's point was this... it was a Connacht final that lay ahead of us and there was nothing to worry about.

Compare that fear or those nerves to the prospect of being dumped from a helicopter thousands of feet in the air... which was what Smith thought was about to happen.

It was one of many memorable Morrison moments but now he's telling us to keep it simple, drilling into us that what we have done in training will manifest itself on the field of play.

Morrison is a firm believer that training ground work will transfer to match day. Perform, and let the result look after itself. If you perform and you don't win... so be it.

There's nothing more you can do after that.

So, what's to worry about to begin with?

Morrison and Moran chat to each of the players individually, wishing them luck... asking if they're feeling okay?

It's all about the game plan.

'Stick to it...

'Be confident...

'Be ready...!'

Psychologically, I think we're in a better place.

In 2004, the occasion got to us more in the build-up to the final. There was a lot of talk the week before!

This time, it's play the game… not the occasion. Two years before, I was wondering what it would be like during the weeks and days after winning an All-Ireland title? The celebrations?

The craic… the tour of the county?

Now, expectation is bigger. It's so close again. We've been knocking on this door for a while now. Beaten finalists in 1996, '97 and '04… surely if we keep knocking, one day, one Sunday soon the door will open?

That's always been the way in Mayo. But the fact of the matter is that the best team will generally win the All-Ireland.

You'll rarely win one hoping that the other team plays poorly and you play well. And there's still an element of that surrounding this game. Mayo fans are hoping that the likes of Cooper, Declan O'Sullivan, Donaghy, Galvin and Darragh Ó Sé underperform, and that some of our players have the games of their lives.

But, any given Sunday, if we're playing a team with superior players in some positions, and if they play well and we also play well… they're still going to win, aren't they?

It's like what you see in the Premier League every week, when the top teams play against the ones struggling at the foot of the table. Leicester City might play Manchester United, for example. Theoretically the only way that Leicester City are going to win that game is if they play one of their greatest ever games… and Manchester United underperform.

And that's how it is with Kerry.

Their team on paper, and on the field if all of their top players all perform right up to par, is superior to ours. That's not me kidding them or kidding with myself.

That's reality.

Still, we have belief.

It's only in the aftermath of big games that you can understand, appreciate and accept that reality. Maybe we could have set out with a more defensive strategy and packed our defence more?

Maybe it is folly to go toe to toe, in a footballing sense, with the best football team in the country. Trying to beat them by playing football isn't always going to work.

The past is the past.

Some people have said that Mickey Moran and John Morrison should be devising a strategy for this final against Kerry, based on *what happened* or *what didn't happen* to us in 2004.

The last thing that Mickey would have wanted to do when he took over was to look back at the John Maughan reign. Instead, he wanted to lay down his own marker, put his own stamp on the team. In a broader sense, perhaps there should have been a proper debrief on 2004, a major sit down and think-tank involving the major stakeholders in Mayo GAA.

The management… players… officials… but there was no debrief. Even if there was, it wouldn't have been genuine. County board and management teams are effectively two different entities.

A County board will strive for what it wants to achieve, a team management the same. It's rare that you'll ever get total honesty and unity.

Certainly not in Mayo, from my experience.

Trevor Mortimer

I'M not a big fan of organised warm-ups, the drill sergeant stuff.

I always prefer getting out on the pitch, kicking a few balls and getting a feel for it. For a forward with the added responsibility of taking frees, I always feel that it is important to get my eye in, rather than taking part in kicking or hand passing drills, especially in Croke Park.

After all, the nitty-gritty business for a forward is kicking the ball over the bar. And nothing else matters, does it?

Looking at a warm-up from the stands, it must look chaotic.

But in fact, it's organised chaos.

One free-taker shooting from the left, another from the right... goalkeepers going through their drills... defenders working on turning sharply.

It's running like clockwork and everybody knows what they're supposed to be doing. It's important for the forwards, in particular, to stick to routine and get their hands on the ball as much as possible in the warm-up. And so when I'm going through a drill, when I reach the back of the line, I'll kick a ball and get back in the line again.

A creature of habit.

***

The warm-up on the pitch is pretty intense.

It's an All-Ireland final.

It's how it should be.

Hands on the ball... then conditioned games with the squad broken into smaller groups. Blood is flowing faster, hearts pumping. We're warming up at the Hill 16 end of Croke Park again, and it's been a lucky end for us this year. And our warm-up before the semi-final victory over Dublin was one of the most talked-about episodes of the year.

There had been no real talk in the dressing room before the Dublin game about warming up at the Hill end. Moran and Morrison had suggested warming up at the Canal End or the Davin Stand side of Croke Park but David Brady was one of those adamant that we'd take the Hill end... sacred to the Dublin supporters... and their team.

We were out first and after the pre-match photograph, we trotted down towards Hill 16, where we were met by a cacophony of boos and jeers from the Dublin supporters massed on the famous terracing.

It wasn't long before all hell broke loose after Dublin emerged from the tunnel to see us warming up down there. And down they marched, arm in arm, to meet us. Dublin's manager Paul Caffrey pushed into Morrison and Austin O'Malley took a box in the mouth from a member of the Dublin backroom team. Brady was stood beside this.

'You f*****g c**t... watch yourself.'

The verbals were flying, and I was giving it to Brian Talty, the Galway man involved with Dublin who would later become my club manager at Parnells in the capital.

It was impossible to get a good warm-up done.

Two squads and two sets of backroom staff in the one area. Our dietician, Mary McNicholas needed treatment on the pitch after she was struck with a football... and it was all a bit much. Dublin's extravagant march was over the top, I felt. A sideshow!

But it got the fans on Hill 16 riled up, that's for sure.

Dublin under Caffrey were like that. Mouthy and not particularly well liked. There was a lot of stuff going on, knees into the body when you were lying on the ground, for example. I hit a wide with my right foot and Bryan Cullen was running out behind me.

'You should be scoring them,' he told me.

I didn't mind that.

It was tame in comparison to the verbals you'd receive from other players during games. And Dublin were never afraid to let you know what they thought of you. Anything to get an edge!

It was funny, I thought, because I'd won a Sigerson with Culley that year. Stephen Cluxton, the Dublin goalkeeper, played on that successful college team with Dublin City University too, as did Paul Casey and Declan Lally. And they're good lads, the Dublin boys. Most inter-county players are.

But now, we're aiming to take our place among the elite. Another chance has come our way and it's almost time to take it.

We can't fail again.

It's been one of those years for Trevor, with injury restricting him to a substitute's role for the most part. He's suffered terribly with hamstring problems but even when he's injured, Trevor's a leader. And as my big brother, he's always looked out for me, always had my best interests at heart. He told me so many times to steer clear of the media, not to be 'talking s***' in the papers.

I hope that he'll come on in today's final because we need him. He's the type of abrasive character that every team needs. Other players will try to avoid contact but Trevor looks for the hit. He was one of our best players in 2004.

He takes his football seriously and defeats always hit him hard. He'll always go very quiet after losing but even though Trevor has had more than his fair share of losses in big games, he gives everything that he has for the dream of winning an All-Ireland title.

We're different characters by nature. I'm sure I puzzle him at times by how I behave but there's never any judgement from Trevor. And he'd never be embarrassed by me, I hope. That was never the way in our house. There's an underlying, unconditional love in most families, even though Trevor and I are not the huggy types with each other.

Trevor rarely does interviews in the press but when he does, he picks his interviewer carefully. When he speaks, he speaks in measured fashion, a bit like Billy Joe Padden.

Trevor is also a remarkable footballer, untouchable at club level on top form. He breaks from that middle third like a train and as he gets older and gains more experience, his accuracy has improved in front of goal. We played together in three county finals, along with Kenneth - junior, intermediate and senior, but lost them all. We've won more games together than we have lost but, by God, did we lose a lot of finals. But for us, the 2005 county senior final against Crossmolina was one hell of an experience.

The three of us, along with other talented players such as Ronan Walsh, Mark Ronaldson and Dermot Geraghty! We had a good side... a very good side but Crossmolina beat us with experience.

Trevor was devastated after that game and you wouldn't know what to say in those situations. He'd work it out with his mates, over a few pints. It's the close ones that would hit him the most, the same as when we travelled to England or further afield to watch Liverpool play.

But he's still one of the first people that I'll turn to with a problem. He's always been my hero... him and Kenneth. Two of the few that I'll listen to.

It's like that when you know people so well. They're my brothers, after all, and I've seen them at their highest and their lowest. I've seen the elation on Trevor's face when we beat Charlestown to reach the county final last year – and how happy he was when Mayo beat Dublin.

Winning an All-Ireland with Mayo would trump any of that though. As it would for all of us! Trevor's come a long way since his senior debut for Mayo in 2000, when he scored three points from corner forward.

But to me he's still the same.

He's still Trevor. My brother.

CHAPTER 14

David Clarke

There's a lot of pageantry and b******t associated with All-Ireland final day. The corporate suits wine and dine behind glass window panes. There's a falseness about it all. It's almost about everything else bar the football. We've tried to avoid the sideshows building up to the game but now, it almost feels like we, the players, are the sideshows.

The din that had greeted us when we left the tunnel and sprinted onto the pitch is indescribable... unquantifiable.

It's not a rush of euphoria, more a loudness in the ears.

For a moment, you forget those nerves for a split second and yet that guttural outpouring of pre-match emotion from the Mayo fans today still doesn't match the noise that greeted McDonald's winning point in the semi-final over Dublin.

That was something else.

And for a player, there's a double-rush.

You know when you kick a ball whether or not it's going over the bar. If it's sailing over, that's one hell of a feeling, but many of the supporters don't realise that you've nailed it until the umpire raises the white flag.

Huge roar.

Huge rush.

After the warm-up I kick a few balls to get the eye in… then… too soon… we're ushered across to meet the President, Mary McAleese.

I'm sure she's a lovely lady and she's been present on Connacht final day before but these formalities are a killer. I'd prefer to be kicking balls over the bar instead of standing around.

Waiting.

Waiting.

It's prolonging the agony and it's not a nice place to be. It's funny… this is what you work for all year but now… that it's here… it's horrible.

Croke Park!

All-Ireland final day!

Surely this is the one place you want to be on the planet?

I do… but… not right now.

We line up behind the Artane Band for the pre-match parade and I try to look straight ahead, focused on the No. 13 of Kevin O'Neill ahead of me in the line. I cast the odd glance into the crowd.

It's difficult to maintain total focus. A water bottle is passed from Kevin to me. I swig from it and hand it to McDonald walking behind me. I look across at the star-studded Kerry forward line walking alongside us.

There they are… Cooper, Galvin, Donaghy, Declan O'Sullivan… a glance that could cripple another footballer… if you let it?

We're drinking water now just for the sake of it, not for the principle of hydration. David Heaney leads us around the four corners of Croke Park before the national anthem. I run towards Hill 16… and I know that it's Tom O'Sullivan who will greet me there.

The Kerry defender is one of the best in the business.

I wish him 'good luck' and he returns the compliment. That's how it should be. It's a habit I've not broken.

Brian Crowe from Cavan is the match referee.

I've never been a fan of his but there have been no specific instructions or warnings from Mickey and John about what he's been picky on during the long summer of games.

It's a big day for Crowe, too. I just hope that he's not overawed by it. Pat McEnaney was one of the greatest referees in the history of Gaelic football but he f***** up in the 1996 All-Ireland final replay.

A mass brawl involved up to 20 players... and yet just two players were sent off. Mayo's Liam McHale was one of them and it proved costly. It was a crazy decision. Colm Coyle of Meath was the other one fingered. Let's hope that there's nothing like that today and that Crowe keeps a tight rein on things.

But he needs his umpires too. I know from experience that O'Sullivan is a cute defender. He'll pull my shirt first... but if I tug his jersey, I'll get nailed for the second offence.

My goal is to ensure that O'Sullivan is on the back-foot right from the start. I don't want to be looking at his No. 4 thundering out of defence with ball in his hand.

He needs to be seeing No. 14.

David Clarke's a monster.

Six feet and two inches tall. And yet you couldn't meet a nicer guy or a more dedicated player. He's our goalkeeper and I've known Clarkey since our Under-21 days.

He's a tough cookie and has had to be to deal with a litany of injuries throughout his career. And he's had to work hard for his place because when Clarkey joined the Mayo senior squad, he had the legend that is Peter Burke ahead of him in the pecking order.

Clarkey's never been one to make major mistakes. He has argued the toss with me when I tell him that he could have done better with a goal scored by Tyrone's Sean Cavanagh in the 2003 All-Ireland Under-21 semi-final. We lost by a goal, 0-9 to 1-9, at Markievicz Park in Sligo.

Cavanagh's goal was the difference. It was a decent strike by Cavanagh, from a long way out, but I felt that Clarkey, given his size and stature, should have prevented it from going in.

But Clarkey learned from that experience and has become one of the finest senior inter-county goalkeepers in the game.

He is a man that you can always rely on, spreading himself big in those one-on-one situations with an opposition forward to pull off crucial saves. He's a traditional, old school goalkeeper, not the type to throw the ball down and *ping* a quick kick-out. Clarkey is more the "boom boom" type, capable of sending the ball 70 or 80 yards from a kick-out.

He didn't start this season as our goalkeeper. He underwent groin surgery in February and played no football at all until he was called in for the All-Ireland quarter-final replay victory over Laois. John Healy, his Ballina Stephenites club mate, came in for a Championship debut against London and also played in the games against Leitrim and Galway in Connacht, and the drawn Laois match.

But Clarkey was always snapping at his heels and when John showed signs of nerves in the Laois game, Mickey Moran opted for change. It was another tough blow for John, who had played in five of our League games in 2004 but he found himself on the outside looking in for the Championship. It has been a remarkable rivalry between the two lads because when Ballina won the All-Ireland club title in 2005, John was in goals for the club but Clarkey was the preferred choice on the county team.

But Clarkey was always up for a scrap, especially with a Mayo jersey at stake. Burke was the obvious challenge when he first came into the county set up in 2002 but when we won Connacht in 2004, Fintan Ruddy was in goal before Peter returned from injury for the All-Ireland series.

In my eyes, he's never received enough credit as a goalkeeper. He's one of the best that Mayo has ever had but Peter Burke was the king, no doubt about it. A colossal figure. We're lucky in Mayo to have had so many quality goalkeepers. And they drive each other on.

***

If I ever score a goal against Clarkey in training, I'm genuinely surprised. And I never score a penalty on him.

He always seems to know where I am going to put it. Clarkey is a guy you never have to worry about. He is vocal on the pitch and his defenders have confidence in him, just how it should be. And right now, I know that we're going to need Clarkey at his very best for the next hour and a bit.

He's one of the main reasons why we've got here but now that the final is here, we're naturally hoping that he doesn't have much to do. A quiet afternoon for a goalkeeper is a good afternoon for a team.

CHAPTER 15

Alan Dillon II

Kerry are signalling their intent.

The game has just started. It's obvious that they're aiming to pepper our full-back line with long, booming deliveries from midfield.

They won the toss.

They wanted to play into the Canal End in the first half.

They won the throw-in too.

Always a psychological advantage.

Then Kieran Donaghy, 6' 5" and all arms and legs, and plenty of ability, moved into full-forward. But we expected that. We knew he'd go toe-to-toe in there with our captain, David Heaney.

Heaney did well with the first delivery inside, however, collecting the ball on our end-line and starting our first attack of the game.

There were a series of hand-passes but we didn't break their lines. Too many passes. They got the turnover.

Paul Galvin, feverishly, hungry as hell, intercepted a loose pass from Ronan McGarrity.

Mike Frank Russell popped the first point of the game over the bar. The game was hardly a minute old. We're on the back foot already.

Trouble. Dermot Geraghty was a long way off Russell.

We lose the first kick-out too.

Kerry come piling in, three players competing for the ball.

Tommy Griffin launches another long ball into their full-forward line. It's a couple of minutes gone and, already, it's an aerial bombardment.

It's old-fashioned stuff but it's effective.

I get my hands on the ball.

First time in my hands.

That's always special... and can spell pressure.

It's hard for a player to forget what he does with his first touch.

Ciaran McDonald angled a pass into my path... and I got there before Tom O'Sullivan.

He pulled me down.

I quickly survey my options... spotted Kevin O'Neill, "Chuckie", free inside. A quick tapped free bounces in front of Chuckie. He lets fly with his left foot... soccer style.

Their goalkeeper, Diarmuid Murphy makes himself big and saves.

Goal chance... gone!

They'll argue, I know already, that I should have tapped the free over the bar... got us on the scoreboard early. I think about that... and try to forget about what they'll say. Goal opportunities don't present themselves in All-Ireland finals that often.

And when they do, you have to take them.

I went for the jugular... that was my instant decision.

The pass might have been slightly over-cooked, but... Chuckie could still have picked the ball up... taken it around Murphy.

Slotted into the net.

It was still a great chance.

I'm happy with my first touch of the ball.

We have possession again.

Another careless hand-pass... this time McGarrity... it's devoured by Kerry. The "Gooch" feeds Donaghy.

He's fouled.

Russell points.

Six minutes gone... we're two points down.

I've had the ball once.

It seems a long time... and Kerry have made the start we wanted... needed. We're under the cosh.

But we're only two down.

Dillo still hasn't touched the ball and he won't like that.

He likes to be involved, pulling the strings and dictating from the half-forward line.

I've seen him get mad in training when things aren't going his way...like defenders tackling him poorly... pulling and dragging out of him.

He has some great battles with Dermot Geraghty in our training games. There is always tension between the two of them and that is good for the intensity of training. These are hard-hitting, tough battles that sometimes spilled over into fisticuffs. And that's how it should be. Ger Cafferky and I have also gone at it few times over the years.

I remember, one occasion, when he was pulling and dragging out of me and I was awarded a free in. That wasn't enough... so I drew across Ger and kicked the two legs out from under him... putting him upside down on his arse.

But I improved marking guys like Cafferky, Trevor Howley, Liam O'Malley and Keith Higgins or just "Zippy". I could score a few points off Zippy and that would fill me with false confidence because Zippy usually cruises in training. He isn't busting his balls. Zippy is a big game player.

And, always, always and forever, Zippy plays well in the big games.

Dillo has himself under pressure to perform today.

He's prepared impeccably. Sometimes it's hard to get into his car with all the empty water bottles strewn around the vehicle. He's looked after himself and worked hard... for days like this Sunday.

Dillo and I will stay friends for life. I'm sure of that. In the earlier years, our contact with each other more or less terminated after the inter-county season until training resumed again in the wintertime. We were *football mates* for want of a better term. Nowadays, we'll ring each other at least every second day.

We still make those trips to the cinema, have the odd couple of pints, head to the shops in Galway. We tog off beside each other. Myself, Dillo and Zippy. We have our seats in the dressing room ... an unwritten rule.

If a new player comes in and sits in our places, he'll be introduced to the order of the dressing room. It is a special place, our dressing room, a place where good friendships have been built.

Long-lasting ones, too... but if we were to win an All-Ireland title... I can only imagine how unbreakable those friendships might become.

Tommy Griffin

Tommy Griffin has started the game like a man possessed for Kerry. After Russell's free, Griffin leapt highest to claim the next kick out... another of those long, hanging David Clarke deliveries.

What followed is utterly devastating.

Sean O'Sullivan fed Seamus Moynihan.

His brilliant, angled ball was collected by Gooch. Declan O'Sullivan arrived to collect a simple pass and... a quick one-two with Donaghy... and... f*** it... the ball is in the back of our net.

It all happened in a blur.

Kerry have cut through us like a knife through... butter... smart, unselfish play from Donaghy. He could have gone himself ... the return pass to Declan O'Sullivan took Clarkey out of the game.

The finish routine.

It's a killer blow.

We're five points down.

MAYO 0-0.

KERRY 1-2.

The scoreboards are like magnets at either end of the ground, shouting at us to look up at them.

Panic stations.

A minute later we're in a more desperate place.

Griffin goes long again... Donaghy makes a magnificent catch over Heaney's head. The finish is brilliant... rifled high past Clarkey.

Two goals.

Two... Kerry goals.

Our world is caving in.

Six minutes... we were two points down.

Two minutes later... we're eight behind.

I haven't scored.

I've handled the ball... once.

This wasn't in the script.

Eight minutes are gone... not that long... a short time ... but eight points. My head is wrecked.

Is everyone's head wrecked?

It's an All-Ireland final day.

Every second counts.

How do we come back?

Can we come back?

We need a score.

We need a goal... no, we need any kind of score!

*F*** it...*

My head is buzzing.

I'm not blaming the full-back line.

The full-back line is being bombarded. The ball is being won elsewhere out the field. There's no pressure at all on the deliveries… and the ball is raining in like scud missiles.

Keith Higgins gets the ball.

It's a bad wide.

The ball goes nowhere into the Hill.

The groan… from the Mayo fans… a giant overwhelming moan that carries the length of the field.

I'd pulled off Tom O'Sullivan… but Zippy decided to shoot. He could have carried the ball forward… a few more steps.

We need a score… to settle.

Desperately.

Any score.

I need to get the ball.

The next ball.

I need to score… it's down to me.

I need to get that first point.

F*** it… I have to get the ball.

I need to touch the ball.

We're f****d.

Jimmy Nallen is gone.

Off.

Substituted … 11 minutes.

I need the ball.

I've got to score.

I've got to stop this.

Jimmy.

One of our leaders… decimated.

On comes another.

A new leader.

David Brady is in… slots in at full-back.

I've never seen Brady at full-back before.

What's Brady thinking?

David Heaney moves to the centre of our defence… where Jimmy was… but…the damage… so much damage has been done.

What's Brady going to do… what's he thinking?

We're not getting any ball in the middle of the field. If we don't get ball in the middle of the field, we've no chance in our full-back line… nobody has a chance… not David Heaney… not Brady… nobody!

Aidan O'Mahony cuts in… another point.

We're 10 behind.

MAYO 0-0.

KERRY 2-4.

O'Mahony is marking Ciaran McDonald.

It's a point that hurts.

It should be O'Mahony on the back foot… not our man.

Thirteen minutes.

Kerry are scoring every time… six from seven or eight attacks. Jimmy's gone… Dermot Geraghty is down injured.

At the other end of the field, I'm waiting for the ball… craving it. I'm looking at the scoreboard at the opposite end of the ground.

MAYO 0-0

KERRY 2-4.

Stop looking… get the ball.

Dillo has the ball.

He hits it cross field… trying to pick me out.

O'Sullivan pounces… gallops away.

Jesus Christ… f*** it.

Sixteen minutes.

I have the ball.

A chink of light. I gather the ball around the 45 metre line. I look for options. There are none… I elect to send a short hand-pass to Billy Joe.

His chip ahead to McDonald falls to Aidan Higgins. He was roaring through from a deep position. Higgins feeds O'Neill.

Goal…!

A goal…!

We have a goal. It's a nice finish from Chuckie. He drew Murphy… slotted the ball in. The exact opposite of his earlier chance..

Brady wins another ball over Donaghy.

The ball is transferred quickly up the field. I take a poor option. I shoot at goal… I'm blocked down by O'Sullivan. I hadn't seen Peadar Gardiner making a good run inside. I wanted to grab my score. My senses failed me.

When I got the ball I felt suffocated.

We were the talk of the country after beating Dublin in the All-Ireland semi-final. It was a game that captivated a nation.

There was our heroic comeback, and Ciaran McDonald's late point. We started to believe the hype. There was talk that some of our players were simply un-markable if they were on their game. If you're listening to all that kind of talk, it's as if you're carrying a giant balloon on your back going into the next game. And if the defender you're marking is good enough, he'll be ready with the pinprick.

Tom O'Sullivan is certainly good enough.

I knew before I ran out onto the field what he was all about, but it doesn't seem to be making a difference. After the 2004 final, I had it in my head that when I got him again, it would be a different story.

It is a different story between the two of us.

Despite the fact that we are being annihilated, I've actually done okay. My aim was that I'd get a few balls and lay them off. Do the simple stuff and work myself into the game. And that's how it's happening. I'm getting the better of O'Sullivan, but what good is that?

Kerry are out of sight.

It's an All-Ireland final. We're here on the biggest day of them all, the Sunday of all Sundays. And I'm half-hoping that the game will be over.

I'm wishing that this Sunday had never begun.

If the ref blows the whistle and ends it all, we'll find refuge. Return to the comfort zone with your mates and a few pints.

We've scored a goal.

But I don't think we're going to come back.

We're not going to win this game. Kerry have more to give. They have just started playing. That's how it is.

We're finished…

McDonald, like the rest of us, is sinking without trace.

Aidan O'Mahony has taken him for a score… it's not meant to be like this. It's supposed to be McDonald dictating the play… arrowing those left-footed passes… and points. He's the only Mayo forward of my generation that I've ever really looked up to. I'm in awe of him.

He's s**t cool with the tattoos… the flashy boots… the tan.

He's different.

One of a kind.

He's not the reason I bleached my hair though.

I had that done in my late teens. I'm a natural jet black.

No… I like McDonald because he's a brilliant footballer. He can almost make an O'Neills size 5 football talk. And he's made me a better player.

Maybe not in other people's eyes, but in mine... there's no doubt!

At club level, a lot of the ball that you get as a corner forward is of poor quality. It's 60-40 or 55-45, rarely 80-20. But with McDonald in our team, he'll telepathically know where you are running. Outside of the left... another *ping* from Mac... turn... bang over the bar. I always score more when he is in the team.

If I get 10 good possessions in a game, with the chance to turn and get a shot off, I'll always fancy myself for five or six points. But when McDonald doesn't play, those figures drop fast. I don't receive the same volume... or quality of ball.

Ciaran McDonald can do nothing to help me this Sunday.

I'm on my own.

The problem is McDonald can't get his hands on the ball.

We're being cleaned out in the middle third.

McDonald is suffering... Mayo are suffering. It's all a far cry from one of the greatest games, if not the greatest, that I was ever involved in. And the point to win that game was McDonald at his finest.

Jesus Christ... it's like that semi-final is years old.

Beating Dublin... I'm now wishing it had never happened.

He is never really a talker... Ciaran.

He'll chat to his own crew but he isn't a big voice in the dressing room. In many ways, he is a shy enough character, reserved. There is an aura about him, too, in the sense that not many people really know Ciaran McDonald.

I think he likes it that way. Some people may think it is an attention-seeking thing but it's simply because he does not do media interviews! It is never a publicity thing as far as I am concerned.

When he plays football, he gets all of the attention that he needs. And no other player in Ireland, in any era, could have scored the point that he did to win the semi-final against Dublin. Not Colm Cooper, not Bernard Brogan... not anybody. Not now, not ever... that tight an angle and to still put the ball over the bar?

A freak score.

One in a million… one in a lifetime.

Take all of the factors into account. His position on the pitch… Hogan Stand side between the 14 and 21 metre lines… and the wind swirling. To nail it with his left foot was incredible. And McDonald had also started that move from inside his own half. The ball went through the hands of Ger Brady, Keith Higgins and Kevin O'Neill before McDonald took possession again and sent over the best ever score at Croke Park. Play 20 others in front of me on a loop on a TV screen and I still won't change my mind.

He is a hard worker too in training but McDonald is naturally fit and strong. He never goes to the gym. He doesn't need to because his day job is laying pipes. When he is in possession of the ball, it is very difficult for an opponent to shrug him off it. The only thing lacking about McDonald, if I am being ultra-critical, is that he doesn't have a right foot. He never uses it. Everybody knows how good his left is and, yet, he isn't predictable. It's very difficult to close down a player that possesses such a combination of skill and power.

We had always felt confident of beating Dublin. We are natural, country footballers. The game was all that we have. In the big cities of Dublin and Cork, they have soccer, hurling, rugby… and then Gaelic football and other sports. But football is everything to us and it's everything to our supporters.

I could see it in their eyes at breakfast time, and again on the streets as the bus made its way to the ground this morning… in the stands and before the game.

But we're failing them again.

And not even McDonald looks like he can bail us out.

CHAPTER 17

Declan O'Sullivan

IT seems like Paul Galvin is everywhere.

The man's a machine, a player I've always admired. He just added another point for them to steal some more of our oxygen. Galvin is symbolic of their style of play... direct, aggressive, hard-running... clinical in every single facet.

I haven't come close to touching the ball for a fourth time.

I'm still counting, and that's not a good thing.

O'Sullivan sees to that, wrapping his arms around my neck as a long ball comes in. He's all over me like a rash.

Donaghy, for the first time, gets the better of Brady in a one-on-one situation. He kicks a point. We're nine down again.

Brady is unlucky. He's never played No.3 in his life... he almost got it from Donaghy... he needs more help, greater cover... our corner backs need to be tighter and closer to him. Would Mike McCarthy be left one-on-one with any our forwards? No way.

It's naïve stuff.

We're thinking like 14 year olds.

***

In the middle, there's still no pressure on the Kerry players.

They are winning everything.

They strike again.

Twenty-six minutes are gone.

Another long ball and Gooch is in behind Zippy. Clarkey makes a good save from the initial effort... touching it onto the post. But Gooch strolls around Zippy... he sees a gap.

Gooch drills the ball low inside Clarkey's left hand post. We've been punished... again... for not working hard enough.

We get a point.

Billy Joe Padden collects a loose ball that bounces off me.

Twenty-seven minutes. I've played a part in both of our scores. Things might not be going our way but I'm still scrapping inside with O'Sullivan, clawing for any inch that I can get.

He's called out by the referee, looking around with disbelief on his face, but he knows! O'Sullivan knows!

'Once... twice... three times!' the ref tells O'Sullivan. He books him. Now, I'm thinking, this could be a good thing.

My man is on a yellow card. The natural tactic now should be to pepper my area with ball. O'Sullivan can not touch me for a while. The tugging and pushing will have to stop for a few minutes at least.

Getting the ball for us in the middle is still easier said than done. Kerry are lording it around the middle. And... any time we get possession, we lose it.

Is it nerves?

What is it?

The game is too long on for anyone to be nervous?

Look at that scoreboard... for f***sake!

I don't know how we're losing ball after ball, but Ronan McGarrity keeps giving the ball away.

Seamus Moynihan runs and fists a point.

They had another goal for the taking. Moynihan and O'Mahony are right up on top of our defence when they should be asked questions at the other end. The squeeze is on.

They are now 12 clear.

They're coming through the middle too easy.

It was a mistake taking off Jimmy Nallen.

The house of cards is falling down.

It all looks so clear to me.

Heaney from full-back to centre... Brady on the edge of the square. The holes are gaping ones and Kerry are killing us with variation. They're going long... short... running at us. Our shape is gone.

McDonald *fizzes* over a free.

It barely registers with our supporters.

Means little or nothing to me either.

I want to disappear into our dressing room.

O'Neill has the ball.

He feeds Pat Harte.

We've scored a goal.

McDonald has the ball in his hands. He tries for his point. The ball comes back off the upright. O'Neill is waiting when the ball drops.

Chuckie bangs it home from close range. We've scored two goals. In 60 seconds we've scored two goals. I've had nothing to do with either of them. I'm as amazed as everyone else in the ground.

I wanted to be in the dressing room five minutes ago. We were 12 points behind... now the gap is... five!

Five points.

I want the ball. I want to score before this half ends and before I get back to the dressing room. I want to score a point... two points. Another score or two before half-time will have Kerry asking serious questions about themselves.

We need to win everything in the middle for every last second of the half. But... Declan O'Sullivan gets on the end of a pass. He shoots an absolutely massive point... as our fans are still settling back into their seats.

Six points down... when we should have been looking to make it four... or three... before being back in that room. I have the ball in my hands again. The half is almost up. Dillo had forced Marc Ó Sé out over the sideline with good pressure but again, I take a wrong option.

I aim for Billy Joe... but the ball is cut out.

The whistle blows for half-time.

MAYO 3-2.

KERRY 3-8.

Six points.

We've scored three goals... and we're six points down. It does not make sense. It's the strangest scoreline I have ever seen in a Championship game. It's the strangest afternoon I've ever experienced in Croke Park.

But we're not out of it. We have to tell ourselves that... even if, deep down, I'm not believing it. I haven't really done a whole lot ... how can I do more?

The hope we carry with us down the tunnel and back into our own dressing room is rooted in make-believe. Kerry fell asleep for a couple of minutes. O'Sullivan's point was a killer. If they had not scored that point?

That's all I can think about as I walk to the dressing room. That O'Sullivan point. If we'd got another... if I had got the ball... turned right... turned back left... and bang... over the bar.

If that had happened.

If I'd scored and we were four points down... just a goal away from grabbing the game by the balls, it would be different.

So different.

18

CHAPTER

Kevin O'Neill

James Horan used to write a weekly article in the *Western People*. On one occasion, Kevin O'Neill was his topic and Horan wondered why Chuckie hadn't been used more by Mayo?

The reasons put forward were injuries, intense competition for places and work commitments. Horan probably had a fair idea because O'Neill replaced him in the drawn 1996 All-Ireland final. But if you look back at that game, Colm McMenamin, Ray Dempsey and David Nestor were three of the starting forwards. It baffles me why Chuckie couldn't force his way in there because he was an All Star as a teenager in 1993.

Chuckie flitted in and out of Mayo panels for years but was something of a forgotten man before Mickey Moran rekindled his inter-county career this summer. I'd heard plenty of talk about Chuckie over the years but didn't know a huge amount about him. What I did know was that he was a hell of a nice fella and my brother, Kenneth would have spoken highly of him.

It just seemed that Chuckie disappeared off the face of the earth for a number of years. He was playing well with Knockmore but still not getting a sniff of the county team. Seems to me that Horan was sitting on the fence in that newspaper column.

Chuckie was training with Na Fianna for a number of years before joining the Dublin club in 2005. It was a good move for him and Na Fianna are a star-studded outfit, with Dublin's Jason Sherlock and Dessie Farrell there, as well as Armagh duo, Enda McNulty and Kieran McGeeney. Chuckie also has a big job in the financial world and he flies all over the world on business. As a county footballer, I find him to be a really good trainer and a bit like Austin O'Malley, his body is a temple. In a social setting, Chuckie is king.

You could be nursing a pint in the bar but Chuckie would have wine or champagne at the table. There are no half measures with this man. He strikes me as a higher class of individual, clever and knows what he is doing. And Chuckie is a very smart footballer... very good for me when he is around. He'll put the ball in my lap for me.

One particular score from the Connacht final, early in the second half, summed Chuckie up for me. We were trailing by a point when he collected a ball from McDonald on the left wing.

A more selfish forward would have aimed for a point but Chuckie sent this diagonal cross-field ball into my chest. I was isolated, one-on-one with Damien Burke and put the ball over the bar. And even though Chuckie might not have been highly rated by previous Mayo managers, John Maughan and Pat Holmes, I rated him in McDonald's bracket as a footballer.

Austy tells a great story about the time when the pair of them were heading home from Dublin to Mayo for training. Chuckie always found it hard to get off work but he made up for lost time in the car, thumbing his Blackberry phone incessantly as the emails came flooding in.

Chuckie was driving an automatic Volkswagen Golf GTI, parked in an underground car park near where Austy lived. Now Austy had never driven an automatic car before but that would soon change. Chuckie didn't like to drive the long distances – he preferred to rest the legs before training. And so, after an aborted takeoff when Austy went desperately close to clipping the pillars as he attempted to reverse, they were finally away.

Chuckie was on the Blackberry all the way to Longford.

It never stopped. But then a text came through informing the lads that training was cancelled. Not good. The lads were none too pleased but Chuckie decided to make the best of a bad situation. They had some footballs in the car and pulled in at a GAA pitch.

They kicked 100 balls each and Austy reckons that O'Neill must have kicked 98 of them over the bar. That was the work done for the evening and that was Chuckie... different class, and with a real aura about him. You wouldn't know if he was being serious or taking the piss out of you half the time, but I like Chuckie's buzz. He looks after himself, eating the right food, drinking the right drinks – and I think himself and Austy buzz off each other in that way. I always hit the middle of the road gyms for a work out but not Austy and Chuckie... they will always go to the David Lloyd gym in Clonskeagh.

And Chuckie has made the most of 2006. Hard to believe that this man had come on as a sub in an All-Ireland final but was then dropped from the squad two weeks later. And yet here he is, after all these years, scoring two goals and making another as we have clawed our way back.

Maybe it's not over yet.

CHAPTER 19

Moran and Morrison

Time to draw breath.

A renewed sense of optimism surges through our dressing room at half-time.

'We can do this.... WE CAN'

If the whistle had blown on the half hour mark, we were finished.

Twelve points down then… just six now.

The two goals have energised us but O'Sullivan's point was crucial for Kerry… after we'd cut the gap to five. We sit there for a couple of minutes, coming down from the high.

Morrison and Moran troop in.

'Ye have a chance… BOYS.

'Ye're BACK… BACK in this… GAME!'

Morrison is all about belief.

Believe… believe… believe.

Do I believe?

Fifty-fifty, if I'm being honest with myself.

Let's put it this way... I don't think we *can't* win the game... but I *can't* see our names up in lights either. I'm not sure if I'm making any sense to myself. It's a strange kind of limbo.

If I was in the Kerry dressing room, six points clear at half-time... I'd believe. I just wonder how Kerry will handle that advantage? They'll either retreat or they'll drive on. I suspect Kerry still have that same unwavering faith in their ability to close things out. Their confidence is still high and they'll play like that. And if we're not careful, they'll get the run on us again... and cruise out of sight.

It's important that we start the second-half well but our first-half stats are poor. They've punished us whenever we've turned over possession and we're doing everything that we spoke about *not doing*.

It's not even the f*****g turnovers. We've misplaced hand-passes and kick passes, and we're carrying the ball into tackles.

So the message is simple.

Stop turning over the ball... keep it... work the chances and take the scores. And stop them running through the middle each time.

We still believe that we can do this.

Stay in the game until 50 or 60 minutes... then we have a chance. That's been our philosophy right through the season and it's served us well. Just be there with 10 minutes to go.

That's what we'd said in the build-up to this game.

In 2004, we had no chance with 10 minutes left but even if we are five points down with 60 minutes on the watch this time, we will still believe that we can win the All-Ireland. But Kerry are scoring more freely and easier than us.

If they have 10 chances, they're taking eight.

If we have 10, we're converting two.

They've been more economical with the ball and they haven't missed much. And their shooting is more relaxed than ours. We're edgy when we get within the scoring zone... myself included.

The nerves are back again now, as bad as they were before the game. Jimmy Nallen, God bless him, tells us to relax and be calm.

Chuckie tells me to keep making the runs and he'll pick me out, like he did with that pass in the Galway game. McDonald tells us to keep working and it will happen. Brady addresses the group and it's inspirational stuff.

'NEVER…NEVER GIVE UP … keep driving… ON'.

Plenty of expletives are thrown in for good measure.

That's DB.

We're in a better position than two years ago. Then we were eight points behind at half-time. It's not much better… but still better.

And we had that bit of momentum before half-time, even though O'Sullivan popped that late score. We've banged home two quick goals… surely it's planted a seed of doubt in their minds?

But Kerry don't do panic.

They might be frustrated but they won't be panicked.

Tom O'Sullivan hasn't said a whole lot. Usually, in other games, he'd let loose with a verbal volley if a forward took a bad option at the other end of the field.

'What the f*** are you doing?'

And that's one of the great things about Kerry. They might be friends, all of them, but they are teammates and they aren't shy about having a go at each other. But Tom O'Sullivan's just witnessed an attacking master class.

No words are needed.

I can't stop thinking about the turnovers.

Are Kerry really that good?

Or are we gifting them this?

The stuff we've worked on religiously has let us down. And unfortunately, on a bad day it's not just one or two mistakes that cost a team… all of the stuff that's built up over the season comes out in one bad game.

That's what's happening to us. Easy turnovers… possession given away… kick-outs lost. Everything's gone against us and we can't beat the best teams playing like that. I whisper a silent prayer to myself before we head back out.

It's one I say before every match, and at half-time.

'Jesus, Jesus… Help Me.'

It's the prayer that George told me. It seems to me that sometimes it works… sometimes it doesn't. It's obviously not working today, that's for sure.

It's been tough out there.

I'm mentally drained already and there's a half left. My head's not completely melted but I'm thinking negative thoughts. I haven't scored yet and I've missed one or two. It's easy to look back and say that I was alright in the first-half… six out of 10 stuff, but in the eyes of the prying public, it's all about bald facts… and I haven't scored. And I'm an inside forward.

*I'm meant to f*****g score!*

It's not the best game I've played by any means but I have to trust in myself and believe that if I keep getting into good positions… it will happen. Just like McDonald said!

But it's very easy to doubt yourself when you're not scoring.

The tunnel awaits us once more and we troop out to face the light. *We might do this yet.*

We have a chance. All is not lost.

John Morrison is the man who generally takes the lead in team talks. But whenever Mickey Moran speaks, I listen.

It wasn't that I wasn't listening to John, far from it, but Mickey has a more calculated view. John is more a free spirit… gung ho… and he has his own particular psychology. This is important in many respects, but Mickey brings a cold, clinical analysis to the table.

A manager's role in situations like this… six points down at half-time in an All-Ireland final… it's hugely important.

When a game is in the balance, a good manager can control and influence what happens in the second-half. We obviously can't go out in the second-half and approach the game like we did the first… because that clearly isn't working. And in relation to turnovers, where we were falling down badly, Morrison is technical in his analysis.

'Use the inside of the boot when passing the ball… not the outside,' Morrison tells us all. That makes sense.

Kicking with the inside of the boot is a safer pass… less margin for error.

Execute that skill incorrectly and you'll lose the ball. But with someone like McDonald, or McDanger as we called him, different rules apply. He is a player, in my eyes, that you can't criticise. He is a huge reason why we are here in the first place and in fairness, he is trying things and working his bollocks off.

McDonald will shoot and ninty-nine per cent of the time the ball will go over the bar. But not today… this is not one of those days.

I don't think that Morrison is off-the-wall, although I'd heard that view expressed before by other players who have worked with him. And I buy into his very special brand of psychology because after a while, listening to him, learning from him, I knew that I was becoming a better player. I was being coached for the first time in my entire career… at 24 years of age. I have John Morrison to thank for that.

With managers I have worked with previously there was no individual coaching. Forwards… backs… midfielders and goalkeepers, essentially we all did the same training. But Morrison works individually with players.

He watches how we play and outlines how he thinks we can improve. Some players like that, some didn't. Morrison felt that I could improve by making better runs. When he and Moran came on board, however, my game was evolving. I was becoming more of a team player, whereas previously I wouldn't have passed the ball a lot. My first instinct was always to shoot and score. But it became apparent during John Maughan's second coming that I needed to change a few things about my game.

There was a time when I was in danger of being taken off if I hadn't registered five or six points but it was only when I got older that I truly realised that it wasn't all about scoring.

Don't get me wrong, I've always considered myself a team player. But it is only now in my career that I have begun to understand what that truly means. And Morrison helped me to understand.

I always trained hard and did what I had to do for the team to be successful. But my role was to score, from play and frees, and as a younger player I might not see the option of the player in a better position. A big part of the reason for that is because I was conditioned to receive the ball... turn... and shoot. But Morrison coached me to look up first to see if there was a teammate in a better position.

If not... take on the man... and thirdly... shoot!

So shooting now became my last option, as opposed to my first. Besides, as my career progressed, defenders were quick to realise that when I got the ball, it was simply a case of turn and shoot. I was easier to read and mark. They could let me receive the ball because I wasn't going to take them on. Defenders never realised that I was playing with a dodgy left knee either. It was cleverly disguised but I'd always turn in a way that would see me pushing off my right leg, and not my left.

Morrison and Moran never knew that I was operating without cruciate ligaments in my left knee. They knew that I had issues with my knee but not to that degree. And it wasn't hampering me.

I've often wondered would I have been a better player if I'd been operated on when I was injured in 2001, but I don't think so. No matter how complex my physical and mental make-up, Mickey has confidence in me, always. He believes in me and that is a huge thing.

After every game he gives me the pat on the back, the 'well done,... you're going well.' He'll sometimes tell me that I am a great player.

Mickey Moran is brilliant for my mind.

Now you can talk about all the sport psychology in the world but the easiest way to get the best out of a player is to tell him that he's the best. Sir Alex Ferguson once said that the two most important words he used during his time as manager of Manchester United were... 'well done.' It goes a long way.

I watch when Mayo players are substituted in big games. Who's shaking their hand on the sideline when they come off? If I was a manager, and one of my players was walking off, I'd always shake his hand and say 'well done.' I'd like to think so anyway.

If the opportunity arose in that moment, I'd pull him aside and explain the reasons why he's coming off... either there, or in the dressing room after the game, or the post-match dinner. Don't let it simmer and don't let it fester.

If the player has come off because he's played poorly, tell him what to improve on and that he'll play next week. It's 30 seconds of your time. The bottom line is that if a player doesn't play well, a manager loses his job. So it's in the manager's best interest to get the best out of his players. It's not the manager's job to talk to the media and tell them how good he is.

Players win All-Ireland titles… not managers.

And Mickey is very good with his players. The big thing about Mickey is that you can never tell if he is p***** off with you.

His demeanour never changes from friendly at all times. I certainly never feel that he is annoyed with me at any time. He never tells me, if he is! I'd known from people in Jordanstown that he was a good coach and got the best out of his players. And this summer, we have come from nowhere to contest an All-Ireland final.

We had a mix and match of a team to begin with… a blend of physical players, skilful players and workhorses. By no means were we a brilliant football team but we did well and management had confidence in us. They have let us express ourselves on the pitch and they regularly asked us questions, like… 'what works for you' or… 'what can you bring to this team?'

Then, their job was to gel all of these ideas together and devise a system that suited and benefited everybody. No easy task. It was a philosophy out of kilter with some of the modern day strategies, where players are asked to sacrifice their attacking instincts to fulfil defensive roles.

You see a good centre forward, for example, that has to drop back and play as a sweeper. You're taking away from the player's natural ability to suit a game plan. And that's fine, if the player is happy with a place on the team. But is that player getting the best out of himself?

I'm sure there are players out there who have won All-Ireland medals - and I'd love to be one of those guys – who look back over a year and think to themselves…'I was okay… but could I have been better?'

All this year, I can't look back and think that I could have been better.

Apart from this game… apart from the All-Ireland final… so far.

From the start of this year my confidence has been high, I've been enjoying my football, enjoying the games, enjoying training. I put it down to the way Moran and Morrison coaxed that out of me. It's all well and good doing well at Under-16, minor and Under-21, but county senior football is a pretty unforgiving environment. It's a difficult game to play and I'm always marking the best players from different counties.

Invariably, I end up being tracked by one of the other team's strongest defenders. And there aren't many better in the business at this time than Kerry's Tom O'Sullivan.

CHAPTER 20

Tom O'Sullivan

Stop turning over the ball... keep the ball... work the chances... take the scores. Stop them running through the middle each time.

We have our orders.

We know what we have to do from the very first minute of the second-half. The game is back on... any second.

I'm back with Tom O'Sullivan.

Kerry win the throw-in.

Eoin Brosnan is on as a sub for Tomás Ó Sé. He's running straight at the heart of our defence. He should score.

His shot strikes the upright... drops into the arms of Keith Higgins.

Lucky break.

That would have been a nail in our coffin. Brosnan went through far too easily... he coasted away from our midfielders.

He's fresh.

Strong... and we've just told ourselves a dozen times in the dressing room that they were not going to come down the middle any more in this game!

***

Play switches to our forward line.

Chuckie is beaten in a foot race to the touchline by Mike McCarthy. Even though Chuckie's scored those two goals in the first-half, McCarthy had the legs on him. He is always deceptively quick... McCarthy... I've had him on my tail a few times.

The start to this half is strange.

Confusing.

Not much is happening. I transfer a pass to Chuckie... he drops a shot short. That's not like him.

I get the ball.

My second quick ball in the half... I do the same as Chuckie.

Jesus Christ...

There's an edginess to our shooting. We're rushing everything. This is more of the same... same as the first-half. Only good thing... Kerry haven't penetrated at our end yet.

I still haven't been on the ball much... when it comes my way, I'm reverting to my natural instinct... having that quick shot. How many times has Morrison told me, option three should be to shoot... not option one!

Kerry make it look easier... they grab the first score of the half. Russell to Donaghy... Donaghy to Cooper... a brilliant score with his right foot into the Hill 16 end.

KERRY 3-9.

MAYO 3-2.

We needed that first score... but it's theirs... first blood. The ball arced over the crossbar... right over the black spot.

It was never in doubt.

So f*****g... easy.

The ball comes into me.

I tussle for it with O'Sullivan. He's all over me again and while it looks like six of one and half a dozen of the other, I feel more sinned against than sinner. I was attempting to hold off O'Sullivan...he's pulled me down.

The referee decides to let play continue... the ball bounces out for a 45. *Good... perfect.* These are kicks that McDonald puts over in his sleep.

McDanger screws it badly wide. He's capable of kicking a ball over the bar from 60 or 70 yards but... today... he can't manage it from 45. He's always such an assured kicker, straight and true.

He turns the ball into a missile.

Brosnan is on the ball again.

Galvin is back inside his own 45 for Kerry.

A machine... that's Galvin.

History is repeating itself and there's nothing that we can do about it. Cooper threatens again... but Zippy sticks with him. Aidan Higgins piles in and meets Cooper with a high challenge.

More lads are running in.

DB follows up with a fair rattle on Cooper... Gooch is taking punishment from all angles. Donaghy arrives on the scene.

He bangs into Brady hard. It's a good man that will get up after being double-teamed but even the Gooch is rattled.

The ref takes the easy option and calls Brady and Donaghy over. Two yellow cards. There should have been just one... for Aidan Higgins. Pull out the No 5... show the yellow... move on.

It's poor refereeing. A yellow card is irrelevant to Donaghy at this stage. It really doesn't matter if he doesn't touch the ball again for the remainder of the game. The damage is done... he's been one of the main wrecking balls.

Kerry know they're on their way.

Wasting time suits them perfectly.

AS a defender, Tom O'Sullivan has a number of attributes. He's physical, fast... a good reader of the game. And he's sticky... damn sticky. He has a lot of confidence in himself as well. All of that combines to make him one of the best corner backs in the business. If you're a player lacking a bit of confidence, you'd struggle with Tom O'Sullivan. He preys on insecurity and thrives on weakness. But he is never mouthy... not to me anyway. I'd hear other players talk about him barking this and that but I never experienced that. Perhaps it's because he never feels threatened... by me?

I've had a pint with Tom a few times. I always found him a good guy, a bit cheeky and a touch arrogant at times but with so many All-Ireland medals in his back pocket, he can afford to be. I think he might have held up his hand to signify how many one night when Trevor was there. I'm not sure that Trevor was best pleased but I never paid too much attention to stuff like that.

I'd like to think that he respects me as a player. I certainly have respected Tom and other corner backs, like Tyrone's Ryan McMenamin. If you respect a player, and you're looking for respect from him, you won't taint yourself by mouthing at him. Niall Bogue... the Fermanagh defender... he's different. In the 2004 All-Ireland semi-final he was non-stop.

I'd being doing well on Ryan McCluskey... then Bogue trotted across to pick me up. He was chatting about this and that... my mother... my grandmother.

I kicked a score and laughed in his face.

That's the perfect riposte to that kind of stuff. Players like that know that they can't better you with football. They struggle to mark you so they'll try something else to beat you. But it's what footballers do on the field and I can't say that I'm whiter than white.

I've never said anything of a deeply personal nature that I regret but I've taunted some of my opponents. I've walked around a defender, kicked the ball over the bar and asked the defender the big question.

'Is that all you can do?'

Or.

'Can you do better than that?'

'You're having a s**t day.'

'Get someone else out here to mark me.'

Silly... silly stuff. The kind of things I said to defenders when I was in my teens, playing Under-16 and minor... go round a guy and come back... around to do it again. And chatting to him while I was doing that.

But I was young then.

I had no real thought process.

There is no way that I'd get away with that kind of stuff against Tom O'Sullivan. I have to get the ball, for starters.

And when Tom has possession, he is good with it. He can carry the ball comfortably out of defence... play the simple pass. But I still believe that I can get the measure of him... given the right kind of service.

Running in straight lines, a forward won't beat Tom.

He's got pace. But moving at angles, there's a chance... if there's diagonal ball coming my way. Tom isn't the best on the turn but he was incredibly pacey coming from behind me to attack the ball.

He always gets the fist in. Now... more than ever... I needed to heed Morrison's advice and make those five or six runs in an attempt to get free. Running in straight lines or in a confined space, I am toast.

Defenders love those straight lines. An odd one might match me on angled balls but only if he's athletic and agile enough. But if you're agile, pacey and can turn... you generally won't be put in as a corner back.

You'll play in the half-back line... centrally or in one of the wing positions. Unfortunately for me, Tom is the kind of player that fits seamlessly into the Kerry full-back line. And he had my number in one All-Ireland final.... and he has it again now, unless...

I did well on him in a League game in 2010... I came on as a sub to kick four points from play but... that means nothing in the greater scheme of things. It means plenty to me but nobody remembers League games. I need to burn Tom O'Sullivan now... right this minute. It has to happen... now.

As an inter-county corner forward, you can always be guaranteed that the player you're marking can *play*. The majority of corner backs are centre backs with their clubs so they can *play big time* on the big stage.

When I started playing junior club football at 16, the corner backs that I marked wouldn't have been the best. But you're a silly man if you're marking a corner back and wondering why he's not in a more central position. Often, corner backs are among the best players on the team.

Donegal have Karl Lacey, Galway have Damien Burke, O'Sullivan in Kerry, Cork have Anthony Lynch. Those are the players I find myself up against. Dublin's Paul Griffin … another excellent player… McMenamin and Conor Gormley in Tyrone… Michael McGoldrick and Sean Marty Lockhart in Derry.

What a player Lockhart is!

A brilliant footballer. Nothing mean about him… just a fantastic player. He can beat forwards with pure football. The one player that I have never got to mark that I would love to test myself against is Kerry's Marc Ó Sé.

He can read the game… and play ball. All of that family are footballers, all the way down from their late, great uncle Páidí. Nice fellas off the pitch but on the field… and I've come across Tomás and Darragh… they are never afraid to give you a clip. I used to love watching Marc play though. He defends supremely and then finds time to pop up with a glorious score.

Different class.

'Ricey' McMenamin is one of those players that opponents love to hate. He is really sticky. Ricey has earned something of a reputation for himself for sledging but it isn't the family stuff with me.

He's a lovely lad… Ricey. I got to know him on an All Star tour and I found him to be great company. Gormley is another tough nut… but I've had some good games against Tyrone. Gormley is the type of defender who can get something on a 50-50 ball and while I have the edge on him for pace, he can read the game and is very strong.

The day will come when I'll look back and reflect upon some of the great defenders that I've marked. And I'll be happy enough with my lot… considering their quality. But it's my own flesh and blood, Kenneth who is probably the toughest f****r than I ever marked.

He was working in Claremorris and playing there for a while but when he came back to Shrule, I had the dubious pleasure of marking him in training. Kenneth was just different class. You could be standing five yards off him but his intuition for where the ball was going to land ensured that he ate up the difference.

Kenneth didn't have to be glued to you to cut the ball out. His positioning was top notch and he could also bomb forward to take a score. He hit hard... but usually within the rules. Kenneth was one of those old school, filthy corner backs but he dished out the hits in a legal way... just about. He played on the edge... real borderline defending. He's not that tall, but Kenneth is built like a brick s***thouse and the thing I loved about him was that he usually marked the best opposition forwards when he played for Mayo.

Marking any of the defenders I've mentioned is always a challenge. But if life was the proverbial bed of roses, there would never be adversity to overcome. I'd probably be standing here with one All-Ireland medal in my pocket... and aiming to pluck a second.

And I'd be a universally-liked fellow.

I'm not at a stage in my life where I'm particularly interested in changing people's opinions of me. What you see, essentially, is what you get. Some people like me... others don't.

I'm not particularly bothered about that.

My dream has always been to play for Mayo and I managed that. I can't do any more. Regardless of what I did or didn't do, I've played for Mayo in minor, Under-21 and senior All-Ireland finals... and I'm going to do everything I can to finish my career as the county's all-time leading scorer in senior inter-county football.

The record is held by Joe Corcoran.

I've played over 100 competitive games for Mayo... could never have dreamed that that would be the case when I was 15 years old.

That scoring record doesn't consume me.

Breaking that record is not something that I've ever dwelled on too much but it would be nice all the same... private confirmation that I've done more right than wrong in my days with Mayo.

CHAPTER 21

Ciaran McDonald

I've been the best part of two minutes standing around at the Canal End goal. Waiting… hoping.

It's a weird feeling.

There's no need for the stuff that's going on… the pushing and shoving… it's wasting time, and we don't have time to waste.

The ball's back in play… the s*** down at Hill 16 is over. Kerry are happy as little pigs in that same s***.

McDonald has a free from the hand.

This will bring us one back… he pulls it wide.

Another… clear indication… if one more was needed that things aren't going our way. McDonald should nail those 99 times out of 100… like that one from the sideline in the Dublin semi-final… split those same Canal End posts.

One of the scores of the year.

Second behind his winner in the same game… I reckon.

We're still seven points down.

***

It's not an irretrievable situation… but I'm not one hundred per cent confident either… not fifty per cent… and that's pushing it. We're winning more ball around the middle of the field but McDonald is taking all that possession… and he's got Kerry lads swarming all over him.

Cornered… a rat in a kitchen.

O'Mahony's on top of him… Moynihan… Russell.

McDonald coughs up the ball… Donaghy transfers to Declan O'Sullivan. He's laid it off to Brosnan. He just steps past Heaney… slots over another massive… massive score for them.

In the head of every Mayo player… it's a killer. Our best player has held onto the ball too long… given it away… another turnover.

Kerry's biggest point yet.

Donaghy's lying on the ground now… killing the game, killing time. Barry Moran is off the bench and is placed on the edge of their square. Trevor is on too. It's route one… from here.

Dillo and Chuckie are gone… we're attacking again. Peadar fists a pass inside to McDonald… he's come roaring in from the left touchline. He's still running… still trying things.

He skews a shot wide on the near side. It's a poor miss. Three points from those three misses … and we'd have been back to a five-point game. We'd have a chance then. Slim… but a chance.

Nothing's going right for McDanger. He's given away a hand pass and Moynihan has charged clear. Kerry are attacking again… coming at us in waves, like they've been doing all game.

They're breaking the line… breaking tackles. Darragh Ó Sé lobs a ball towards Cooper… he's a long way from goal. It's a slow, methodical build-up but the clock is with Kerry.

They can do that… they're so far ahead.

We have the ball.

Hartey drives a *hit and hope* towards our end. It's picked up by Brosnan…

he's driving forward.

Trevor pulls him to the ground.

Trevor's booked. The game's dead now... finished.

Kerry are eight clear.

KERRY 3-10.

MAYO 3-2.

The Fat Lady is clearing her throat.

Operation nightmare is in full effect.

Moran and Morrison are helpless on the touchline.

This is an avalanche... a Kerry master class. I'm not sure even Morrison, with all of his positivity, saw this one coming.

He told us during the year to eat Brazil nuts as a snack.

'If you start eating these during the day, you'll start thinking like Brazilians... and you'll play like Brazilians,' he said. That was Morrison's psychology.

Eating them didn't bother me.

I liked them anyway.

I've also been told about the time he brought a big skip to training, one of the ones you'd dump rubbish into if you were clearing out a house.

Morrison placed a ladder on each side of the skip, and a plank across the top. The idea was that you would walk up the ladder, empty your negative thoughts into the skip as you marched across the plank, before coming down the ladder on the other side with a head full of positivity.

It was different and I liked it.

Quirky maybe, but innovative.

I've also heard the rumour from Armagh that he taught their midfielder, Paul McGrane how to field the ball better by using balloons. That's Morrison. He thinks outside the box, but he has a scientific mind too. He brought urine testing into our set-up for the very first time. If our piss isn't the required colour before training, we don't train because you we're not adequately hydrated.

I think he got that one from American Football.

But nothing can save us now. How can anyone tell a player... eight points down against Kerry in All-Ireland final... only 20 minutes left ... that he's going to win the game?

No chance.

Hartey's still pumping the legs at midfield.

I admire him for that. He's a good lad. We've soldiered together for many years. Good craic... but a serious streak in him too. Like the other Ballina lads, there's no badness in him. They have a reputation for being tough but they are good footballers who hit hard.

They aren't the kind of guys to mouth off during club games... narking away. They respect you as a player, give you the hits and take them in return. Hartey and I are good friends. Things aren't going his way... not even a verbal volley will turn it around for him.

Because Hartey is like that. If a manager is giving him grief, that verbal volley only serves to inspire him.

A kick in the arse can see Hartey catch a ball over the head of an opponent five inches taller... followed by a solo down the pitch and a cracker of a goal to cap it off.

That's the kind of player he is... we need to annoy him to get the best out of him.

There is a quiet side to Hartey too. He's come out of his shell a bit with his own friends but he seems reserved before most of the big games. He sits there in the dressing room, alone with his thoughts mostly... doesn't matter whether it is a challenge or Championship match... Pat is the same.

Colm Cooper

Peadar tries another lateral hand pass.

He's in a good attacking position but Trevor and Ger Brady get in each other's way. Trevor runs to try and make the best of a bad situation.

Ger throws his hands in the air… mad as hell.

Another heartbreaking turnover. Gooch catches a high ball over Higgins… turns him inside out…lofts over a beautiful left-footed score.

I can't believe he's just done that… *how he's just done that?*

I feel like applauding. It's the type of point I can only dream of today. McDonald tried to get in a challenge as Cooper got his shot away.

McDonald… at corner back?

It doesn't add up.

Billy Joe walks off… shaking his head.

Aidan Kilcoyne is on.

"Killer" has been coming good… scored 1-6 when Mayo won the All-Ireland Under-21 final earlier this year. He's a promising talent but… what's he going to do out here?

Galvin wrestles Trevor to the ground. Trevor leaves a calling card and digs his knee into him. My first point of the game?

Ball in hand... I'm nervous.

Kerry defenders are shouting... 'POST... POST...!'

That stuff annoys me... I'm more annoyed that I'm hearing them. But it's still a free I'm expected to tap over the bar from 20 metres.

It creeps... just... inside Diarmuid Murphy's left hand upright.

I breathe out.... finally off the mark... something... but it means nothing.

I look down the other end of the field. There's Cooper... waiting... not a worry in the world. I guess that's how he's feeling... I know I'll never get to feel how he does right now.

He's been team captain for part of the year ... he's already expecting to lift Sam Maguire. What a load to share?

He was the Texaco Footballer of the year in 2004 ... this'll be his second All-Ireland senior medal. He or Donaghy will win the Footballer of the Year award... funny... my odds for that individual honour were slashed after the quarter-finals.

They're back in the big numbers now...

Kerry base their game around maximising Cooper's talent. And if I was Jack O'Connor, I'd do the same the whole game.

It's a no-brainer. Do whatever you have to do to get the ball to him in his area... every game. Do that... Kerry win every time. Sounds simple but that's what they've done.

I know it has taken them an awful lot of hard work on the training ground.

But Donaghy's switch to full forward during the Championship has been the masterstroke... what a partner he is for Cooper. I'd say Gooch gets at least ninety per cent of the final passes that reach that inside line. That's how it seems, anyway. He's been immense.

But, on top of that... Cooper has that great awareness... and the ability to get himself into a position where he can take the ball and shoot... instantly. His first point of the second half was all of that... strikes me that Cooper's mind works 10 times faster than mine on a football pitch.

Cooper doesn't generally get the ball… beat his man with speed… run in on goal and kick the ball over the bar. Nah… he gets the ball… turns and shoots, because he has already bought that space for himself.

Left foot… right foot, it doesn't matter. He's deadly. One of the best players that I've ever seen… the best corner forward of all time, and I don't think we'll ever see a player like him again.

I've played senior inter-county football for a long time…been marked by some of the best defenders in the country and have had the s*** kicked out of me. But Cooper received the same, if not worse… all the time from defenders. He's the best player on the pitch every Sunday.

He's made to suffer because of that. And yet he's won his All-Ireland medals… All Star awards…. everything… it's phenomenal. The guy just wants to play with the same innocence… beauty a kid shows when he first picks up a football. That's Gooch. That's how he survives it all… I think anyway.

They're just a different breed in Kerry… aristocrats of the game… to begin with… and forever.

A Kerry footballer's gauge is the amount of All-Ireland medals that he's winning. If Cooper never won an All-Ireland, he'd still be regarded as a star at national level but not so much within Kerry.

All-Ireland titles define players in Kerry.

With us… in Mayo it's the lack of All-Ireland titles that define us. What we give or gave to the cause is secondary… because we haven't won the biggest prize of all. A few of us have been lucky enough to win All Stars. But it's not worth a f*** really. We're floundering again at the big house.

And Cooper is busy adding to his legend.

Our corner backs Dermot Geraghty and Keith Higgins were the men handed the unenviable roles for this final. Their missions… and they chose to accept them… were to keep tabs on the Gooch and Kerry's other corner forward, Mike Frank Russell.

I never thought of Keith as an out-and-out corner back but he's shown that he is one of the best footballers in the country. Zippy relies on his speed, which would have made him a better fit in the half back line… in my view.

But Zippy was always one of our best players in the vast majority of our games. He rarely plays poorly… even if his direct opponent isn't scoring, he'll still contribute to the game by bombing forward… setting up scores… popping over the odd one himself.

A very unassuming kind of guy… Zippy.

Down to earth and a class hurler too. Hurling is his first love. Ballyhaunis introduced hurling into their club a few years before Zippy was born and his father was big into the game. Zippy might train with us on Saturday mornings and he'll be off later that evening or the next day hurling with club or county. He has this endless energy about him.

He was never big into lifting weights, he didn't need to be because he's strong… tough and wiry.

And he's a great character in the Mayo dressing room. He's a guy Mayo footballers look up to and respect. More than anything he's a fabulous footballer. I love marking Zippy in training because I'm testing myself against the best.

I rate myself against the top footballers and Zippy is one of them… always will be.

Colm Cooper is too hot to handle, though.

Not too many defenders have managed to stop him. He's not the type of player that you'll encounter in the Connacht Championship or in an All-Ireland quarter-final. Zippy is finding out all about that today. Zippy is faster than Cooper but… Gooch is feasting on that regular, quality supply of ball coming his way.

And that's why I think… still… that Zippy should be in the half-back line. He's played a bit there but not a lot. He's pigeon-holed in the No. 4 shirt… but he could be doing so much more for us.

It didn't really matter who we put on Cooper to begin with!

Jack O'Connor is a clever man. He pinpointed Zippy as one of our main players. He's happy to have Gooch on Zippy… he knows that has a two-fold effect.

Zippy has enough to think about with Cooper and that doesn't afford him the licence to get forward. Cooper is pacey and classy… and Kerry are happy to pepper that corner of the field.

I'll never understand why football managers look at a team and work with the forwards, backs and midfielders as one unit. They don't work on individual positions… they don't sit down with their selectors and talk about their goalkeeper… their No 2, or 3 and 4… and so on.

It's always about our full back line… our half back line… our midfield, half forward line… full forward line. Units are fine but within every unit there are better players. There's a better corner back on one side than the other. Question is… how do you bring the weaker individual up to the same level as the player in the other corner? That's in-depth coaching… ticking more boxes, and it takes a lot of time to do that.

Our other corner back is Dermot Geraghty, my club mate … from Shrule-Glencorrib. And Dermot's having a good game, despite what's happening down there. Russell's only managed one point from play and he's struggling.

Dermot was on Cooper too for a spell and Cooper lorded it in the air. That surprised me. One of the criticisms people make about Dermot is that he is too small… Cooper's not that tall either… but he's bigger than you think.

I was sitting with Dermot many years ago outside my Granny's house, on a tractor… chatting to him about what he needed to do to make it as a senior inter-county footballer. He was still only in his late teens at the time but itching for his shot. Dermot didn't have that confidence in himself back then to go the extra step but when he got his chance, he took it… he also went very heavy on the weights.

Dermot is one defender you never like to mark.

Dillo always has it awful tough in training against him. They tend to flake the s*** out of each other… but Dillo rarely gets the better of him. And when we get together with Galway, Dermot usually gets the better of his man. When we put Dermot up against a quality forward and his head is right… it's no problem to him.

He hates being beaten… he despises a player getting a score off him.

I've seen him in the past… beating his chest… damning himself.

The 2004 All-Ireland final was a difficult experience for Dermot. He was marking a red-hot Gooch... got taken off at half-time. Cooper scored a goal in the first half of that game... a superb solo effort, and that knocked Dermot for six.

Like all players, Dermot thrives on confidence. And that magical ingredient is often the difference between success and failure at inter-county level.

The margins are so fine.

A man can have more football but be low on confidence. Another man might not be as good but might be high on confidence. It comes to a trial game... the man low on confidence coming into it wins the first couple of balls... and the other man's goosed. One man gets on the panel, the other is turned away.

That's how fine the margins are.

Dermot generally has plenty of confidence.

It has helped him survive in this game.

I was confident of Zippy and Dermot looking after Russell and Cooper.... that's how I was all week... and this morning.

We'd been conceding low totals all year... just 3-67 conceded... in six matches, averaging out at under 13 points per game.

But Cooper's having a particularly good game and Russell did his bit, I suppose. It is job done as far as Jack O'Connor is probably concerned.

CHAPTER 23

David Brady

We've resorted to just lumping the ball in.

We're looking for Barry Moran at full-forward. It's a desperate tactic...
one we hoped that we didn't have to resort to. Kerry have not deviated all day
long but, then again, they don't have to.

Jack O'Connor has got it spot on alright. I know that he's big on targeting
three or four players on the opposition team... working on nullifying their
influence. If Kerry take those players out of the equation they know they're
halfway to winning the game.

That's how it's worked on us.

Dillo's gone off.

McDonald's having a nightmare.

I haven't been in the game either.

I reckon O'Connor is delighted with the number done on Keith Higgins
too.

David Heaney's now on Cooper ... he's doing well on him. But it doesn't
matter now... the game's gone... over... done with.

We've another defeat... another lost All-Ireland to live with... nothing
else to bring home with us.

***

And yet DB is still powering on.

He's thundering into tackles... refusing to accept his fate.

But with 15 minutes left the miracle's not happening. It's the same as 2004... hoping, praying that a spark might ignite... something.

No sparks.

McDonald delivers another ball inside to us.

It's s****... useless.

I shouldn't be blaming him... it's wrong to keep looking in his direction... thinking he's let us down.

He couldn't have a worse game if he tried.

O'Mahony rubs salt into the wounds... his second point.

When things go wrong in Croke Park, it's very easy for a terminal malaise to set in. Everything is magnified.

Another thing about Kerry that keeps hitting me ... their players just trot back into position after inflicting each painful wound. No fist pumping... they just get on with it. O'Connor wants to win this game, that's not in doubt now in any event... but he wants to win it well.

There's a cold, calculated streak in the man.

He surrounded himself with class... proven winners. Pat Flanagan is one of the country's finest fitness coaches and then there's his selectors... Johnny Culloty with five All-Ireland senior medals and Ger O'Keeffe, one of the famous four-in-a-row team of 1978-81. O'Connor may not have played for Kerry but that hasn't stopped him becoming a successful coach and manager.

The key is his delegation. With Culloty and O'Keeffe there, O'Connor has shielded himself to an extent from the cynics who might hold that lack of inter-county playing experience against him. Moran and Morrison... our boys?

They're a capable duo in their own right... with plenty of inter-county experience under their belts, but they don't have that quality of back-up... like O'Connor has in spades.

That's left them vulnerable.

Left us all on the edge before this final even started.

***

'This defeat is going to hurt David Brady bad.

He's a survivor from 1996 and '97... a player I revere. Back then, Brady was an animal, a block of a man. Still is now. As my career progressed and I got to know him... I liked that he respected me.

It's been brilliant training with a hero of mine... but it comes with a health warning. In a 50-50 challenge with Brady, he'll cut a man in half. There no half measures. Brady is all in or... nothing in.

I don't know if he ever lifted many weights but his physique is exceptional. And he's the big voice in the dressing room. Brady is also a good trainer.... it's not all talk. He was just 22 when he appeared in his first All-Ireland senior final but while he was still just a boy, he quickly became a man. Brady played in a team of giants.

At least that's what it seemed like to me at the time. Kenneth mightn't have been the tallest but he was wide and strong. And although Jimmy Nallen wasn't a beef-cake and was slight enough... he had that pace to burn. And Nallen was a machine... the fittest footballer in the country.

My relationship with Brady has grown stronger with the passing years, as I became a more senior member of the panel. We have the craic and the odd pint or two. In the early years I never drank so I wouldn't be out after games. To get to know a person from another club properly on a county panel, a few pints can help.

Get drunk with a lad... loosen out... and talk s****.

That's important. You can't form that bond in training, playing games or sharing a hotel room. Brady has a wild streak but he thinks I am mad too.

I have the flashy boots and the hair... whereas Brady doesn't give people any warning that he's different.

His madness really manifests itself on the pitch.

He scored three points against Tyrone in 2004 and at half-time our selector, George Golden told him to sit back and preserve some energy.

Brady went nuts.

'I'm not sitting back... I'm driving into these boys,' he roared.

And he did. After the game John Maughan insisted that Brady apologise for being disrespectful. It was just another moment in a deteriorating relationship that would see Brady retire after 2004... before he was coaxed back by Morrison and Moran for this season.

There are other classic Brady moments... like the time he kissed Galway's Niall Coleman on the check during the 2006 National League semi-final. I've no idea why he did that... we didn't know that he had... until we saw the pictures in the paper the next day.

But it was good to have him back and while I wasn't privy to the personal relationship, or lack thereof, that existed between Maughan and Brady, it was sad to see things end like that for the pair of them in 2004. Deep down I suspect they respected each other but Maughan made some big calls with Brady, leaving him off the 1997 All-Ireland final team and dropping him for the semi-final replay against Fermanagh in 2004.

Brady, like myself, likes speaking to the media and what he says is generally reflective of the mood in the camp. His words always capture the essence of the squad and, in my mind, he has earned the right to express his views.

I'm sure it must have been a difficult moment for Brady when Maughan returned for his second tenure because one of Maughan's selectors was Liam McHale... a club mate of Brady's in Ballina.

Brady and McHale were teammates in 1996 and '97... and suddenly McHale was telling Brady what to do. Here were two men who had played together for God knows how many years at club level. But while Brady had his issues, when he was committed... he was one hundred per cent committed. He trains like he plays.

There are plenty of scrapes in training and Brady isn't averse to fisticuffs. Neither was Maughan.

'Let them at it... let them solve it themselves,' seemed to be his belief.

Brady's first outing this year was the drawn game with Tyrone in the National League in April. He came on a sub in that game and made another appearance off the bench against Galway.

Brady was used from the bench again when we began the Championship with a comfortable victory over London in Ruislip but he broke a bone in his foot on a training camp in Portugal and his next taste of competitive action wasn't until today.

Brady was pushing hard for a starting role but Ronan McGarrity and Pat Harte were a settled pairing... and young.

Not being involved from the start didn't knock back Brady's craving for an All-Ireland title... he was just like the rest of us.

We've all ached for it.

It's the ultimate goal for each and every one of us.

Brady might not have liked not playing, but he's still been utterly committed to the cause. He realised that to get on a county panel in the first place is hard, to get on the team even harder. To win a Championship game is harder again... and to claim a provincial medal is more difficult than that. There's a lot of hurdles to jump... before you get within touching distance of an All-Ireland title... never mind winning it.

Nobody gets picked off the street to play for his county and young players are coming through and pushing for places... all of the time. That's how it has to be... but DB's injury cost him his big chance of starting every game for us.

He'll drink hard tonight after losing this one.

Even though the pain of that defeat to Meath in '96 must have been harder to take. We were hosed in 2004 and 2006 but Mayo lost that All-Ireland in '96... threw it away. They were six points clear in the second half of the first game. And that's why it's a wasted exercise in many respects, comparing and contrasting the final defeats of 1996, '97, '04... and this.

In the last three, we couldn't say that we had a hand on it... that we could have won any of them. But in '96... Jesus, it was there for the taking.

I'll never forget the replay... standing in the Canal End after getting the bus up to Dublin from Shrule.

I went onto the pitch after and marvelled at the sheer size of the place through a haze of disappointment. The posts were huge and all I wanted to do was kick the ball between them. Just for the thrill of it.

Kenneth was devastated and I felt desperate for those boys. They had worked so hard. The training we did with Maughan in 2004 compared to what he had done in the mid 90s was different. But I wouldn't imagine that it was half as difficult as what Maughan put them through in his first spell in charge.

As the years advanced, there has been more of an emphasis on skill.

But Brady can play... compared to plenty of other big Mayo players who were manufactured footballers. McHale was huge too but he possessed natural footballing skills. He had that hand-eye coordination from basketball and was a really silky player. And he had the intelligence to know when to pass, when to play the give and go.

Kerry have that pureness... that's why they're destroying us in this final.

Tomás Ó Sé... Darragh Ó Sé... Eoin Brosnan... huge men and skill to burn. They're the perfect fit for Kerry and capable of playing that high-octane game.

Natural footballers.

Darragh Ó Sé loves the quick hand pass... he takes the return and slots the ball over the bar. He has those quick hands and he's adapted as his career has gone on. You can't play senior county football like you did when you were 19 or 20 years of age.

If you're an excellent player at that young age, the chances are that you'll become a senior player for the guts of 10 years... but the question you need to ask yourself is... whether or not you've become a better player?

Are you class now?

Are you one of the best in Ireland?

And a lot of players won't be. They make a senior squad in their teens and think they have it made. They sit in a comfort zone and stall... unless they're prepared to work hard. Like Darragh.

DB has worked hard at his game but he'll almost always kick the ball with the outside of his boot. It is the only way he can... because he is conditioned to do so. Five times out of 10 it will work but... the other five occasions it won't.

Darragh can do it both ways, inside of the boot or outside... doesn't matter. Galway's Kevin Walsh is a player who can't kick at all with the outside of his boot. If Kevin landed a point from 40 metres, it was a huge punt that just about dropped over the bar. His All-Ireland winning midfield partner, Seán Ó Domhnaill was the same. The skill sets are higher now.

Brady has made the most of what he has as a footballer. I'd have the same respect for him now as I would for Chuckie and McDonald. He's DB… the same footballer that I found it a little bit difficult to talk with at the beginning because of the respect that I had for him. I often wondered did he think that I was a f*****g eejit? As a young whippersnapper, a pat on the back from Brady could lift me 10 feet in the air. Just a handful of players had that effect on me.

Andy Moran

Grandad George isn't here but the rest of the family are.

Kenneth's looking down from the stands... agonising... I guess... in yet another defeat. He's been here... he'll know how it feels for me.

I'm already wishing that the game was over... so we can get the f*** out of here.

Cooper's getting more stick.

More unnecessary stuff.

Brady and Declan O'Sullivan are stuck in each other... plenty of pushing and shoving. But I need the ball.

When is this going to end?

Andy Moran comes on... Peadar drags his body over to the touchline and sits there... clutching his calf. A glance downfield confirms that our shape is gone.

One half forward... two inside.

Everybody sitting back.

Why?

***

Galvin's name ends up in the book and he accepts it.

He's a slight lad but in the coming years he'll fill out to become a beast. Aidan Higgins leaves a calling card on Galvin... Higgins' name goes in the book. It could have been his second yellow... he was lucky after that high tackle on Cooper earlier.

Kerry take off Mike Frank... bring in Bryan Sheehan.

The game is *stop start* now... petering out.

They're champions again... *f*** it*. They could slow it down even more if they want to... *they won't*.

They see more scores for the taking.

That's the Kerry way.

They'll play to the end. It's what their supporters demand. And the opinion of their supporters matters. If they're calling for change... or unhappy with the style of play employed by the team... you can always be sure that it won't be long before the manager reacts.

Their supporters really do have a voice.

Sheehan kicks a free.

KERRY 3-13

MAYO 3-3

There's seven minutes to go. Trevor is dumped on his arse by Marc Ó Sé... he apologises for the poor tackle.

Respect.

He knows he's been clumsy and he taps Trevor to acknowledge it. That's true class. Aiden Kilcoyne has the free on the Cusack Stand touchline. I assume he's going to go short. Instead... he kicks for a point.

There's not enough on it... drops short anyway. Barry Moran doesn't show enough heart going for the ball. They clear their lines... I haul down Declan O'Sullivan. It's a poor challenge... a challenge of a loser.

I walk away from the scene of the crime.

F*** this.

***

Ballaghadereen have produced some cracking footballers down through the years. Sean Mangan… James Kilcullen and Stephen Drake were talented boys, all of a similar age.

So too is Andy Moran.

In terms of raw talent, Mangan's work rate wasn't what it could have been. He was a fine player and brought into Mayo senior panels during the early part of the last decade but he couldn't hack it. Training was tough and he suffered with injury.

Some players are made for county football… Andy is one of them.

It took him a while to make his mark but what really kick-started Andy's career was Sigerson Cup success with Sligo IT. Martin McHugh was manager and a host of Donegal players featured in 2004… the goalkeeper Paul Durcan, Christy Toye, Kevin Cassidy and the McGee brothers, Eamon and Neil. From Mayo, Aidan Higgins played at corner back and the county was also represented by Pat Kelly, Pat Harte, Austin O'Malley and Michael Moyles.

Last year, Sligo IT retained the title, again beating Queen's University. Andy was a sub on the team that won the 2004 final but he started in 2005, along with Keith Higgins, Colm Cafferky and Moyles. Donegal still had Durcan, Eamon McGee and Toye involved… it was a golden period for Sligo IT.

But it was those early wins that gave Andy belief in his own ability. On top of that, he was lifting weights to the extent that he was quickly becoming massive. I'd assume that somebody had a quiet word in Andy's ear and told him to ease off pumping iron because if he could find the right mix of mobility and bulk, he was in business.

A manager's dream is the best way to describe Andy.

He'll do everything the manager says and some people have said that he is a bit of a lick. He'll always be talking about something and asking questions. That's fine, don't get me wrong… just hearing him constantly rabbiting on wasn't for everyone.

Andy has struggled to get into the team… he came on as a sub in the half-back line in the Dublin semi-final. Andy is not really a prolific scorer at county level. He'll score freely at club level but while Andy will never score five or six points from play for Mayo, he can take a good goal when the chance presents itself… like it did against Dublin.

For me, Andy is a more natural half-forward. He's been a solid player right through from his days in the underage ranks and his attitude to the game is top class. He'll have the recovery shake after training, use the ice-baths… always look after himself, at least as professionally as you can do in an amateur setting.

We have a good relationship too.

CHAPTER 25

Paul Galvin

Final five minutes.

Ball in hand again.

Free in.

What do I do here?

Go for a goal with five on the line?

I tap it over.

Head down. I feel like a condemned man but no matter how bad it is… we must keep going. Eamonn Fitzmaurice replaces Tommy Griffin on the Kerry team. Another monster… a huge man.

Kerry are home… they know it. Diarmuid Murphy is taking his time over the kick out and I think back to that early save from Kevin O'Neill… from my quick free. That was crucial.

Kerry open up again.

Three minutes to go… *thanks be to God*!

Declan O'Sullivan thunders through the right side of our defence… kicks a majestic left-footed point. It's fantastic running with just a few minutes to go…really powerful. But I suppose it's easy to look so good when you've another All-Ireland medal in your pocket.

But O'Sullivan has been really good… all day… not exceptional… but still he's going to finish up with one goal and two points. He scored the first goal of the game and kicked that point before half-time… following our two-goal burst.

And that's the hallmark of good players… they come up with the big scores. He's covered so much ground to kick that point and… Christ, even if it was a close game I wouldn't expect him to be moving that well at this stage.

Our subs have failed to make an impact.

Andy's not touched the ball yet… 'Killer' had the free and dropped it short when he was kicking for a score… and Barry's been anonymous on the edge of the square. Eoin Brosnan came on to kick a point for Kerry and he's not finished yet… and Bryan Sheehan added a free after coming in. Small things… big differences in a 70-minute game. Trevor also came on for us and he's still going… still tackling hard.

But Kerry are unstoppable.

I find myself tracking back to our 20 metres line at the other end of the pitch… chasing Sheehan. It's all gone scrappy now.

We win possession… I'm surrounded but still manage to get a pass away to Dermot. Donaghy fouls him … he aims a rabbit punch to Sheehan's midriff.

It's going crazy and stupid.

Just get us out of here.

All of our forwards are back in our own half… there's nobody up front. We cough up the ball again… Donaghy launches an absolute boomer from a long way out. It's dropping… dropping… dropping… over the bar, sneaking in from David Clarke's left hand upright.

When it's your day… it's your day.

Donaghy punches the air. He's just landed a skyscraper, a hit and hope. They just can't miss.

The clock ticks into stoppage time.

Aidan O'Mahony trots off… job done… smile on his face. He's been superb but so too have Galvin and Cooper... too many of them. Andy touches the ball for the first time... but he didn't come on at corner back!

He was brought in to play in the half-forward line.

We're all over the place.

DB pings an aimless ball into enemy territory... Moynihan sweeps it up.

He gives it away... but Barry's on the back foot inside.

Kerry sweep clear again.

They want to keep pushing on and their kicking and ball retention... it's all close to brilliant.

Brosnan barges past Dermot.

He advances through on Clarkey... he saves. The ball squirts back to Brosnan and he chips it... off the ground... back over Clarkey's head.

That's surely the last cut.

I pray it is.

We have another free.

McDonald tells me to put it over.

I shape to have a go... Kerry lads are blocking the route to goal... even now. I take a second glance... it's not on.

And so I tap it over.

Jack O'Connor is still moving on the touchline... on patrol. A posse of photographers move with him... ready for the money shot at full-time.

There could be more suffering.

Moynihan pops the ball to Galvin... he's clean through on goal.

The referee's full-time whistle puts us out of our misery.

It's finally over.

But we're not really out of our misery.

We're not even halfway through.

I shake hands with Tom O'Sullivan... congratulate him on a job well done. Hands up... he's had my number again.

Some of the other Kerry players commiserate.

I break up other small pockets of green and gold celebrations... pass on my best wishes.

No complaints.

I can't say that just one of their players was the difference... that's what makes them great. It wasn't just Galvin... or Cooper or Declan O'Sullivan. It wasn't just Diarmuid Murphy in goal...Tom O'Sullivan... Moynihan. The five Kerry players replaced had all played their part. Tomás Ó Sé was injured but had been quietly effective before going off at half-time. Sean O'Sullivan has been really good... Russell scored his couple of points. Tommy Griffin was solid... fearless in the tackle... and Aidan O'Mahony could be Man of the Match.

Five players that would have made it into our team!

The one man I'd always want to have in the trenches is Galvin.

I really like this guy and I believe that if we had him and Cooper in our teams for 2004 and 2006... we'd have won two All-Irelands. Galvin's my kind of bloke. He's different... has that mad streak in him and doesn't give a f*** what people think. Works his b******s off too and has been a phenomenon for Kerry today.

He's often seen the red mist in his career but with everything else he gives, what's wrong with that... small price to pay.

We don't have a player like him.

He is priceless. Early in the second half David Heaney charged into the Kerry half but Galvin got back... won the ball... and was fouled. Up he got... straight away to restart play.

Kerry were on the front foot again. That's invaluable stuff.

I think his Championship average is one point per game... that's what he's also done in the final, but scoring is secondary to his main role. Galvin understands that well and sticks to what he is good at... getting up and down the pitch, making tackles, winning breaking ball... and giving it to the scoring forwards.

He has come a long way since his days getting picked at wing back for University College Cork.

Up and down... up and down the field... never stopping. The size of his quad muscles... Jesus... and his shape. He is a magnificent specimen...

powerful, fast and strong.

What he has brought to this Kerry team is equally as vital as Darragh Ó Sé or Cooper, Tom O'Sullivan or Declan O'Sullivan. Galvin is such a vital cog and when he doesn't play, Kerry aren't the same team. He relishes responsibility and is a *big game* player. And playing for Kerry really means everything to him.

I can't say a bad word about the fella.

I met him in Dublin a few times and he can let his hair down too. There was this promotional gig... and the lady from the company organising the event rang and asked if I wanted to stay in a hotel the night before? That sounded good to me, a bit of comfort compared to the college digs... a couple of pints and off to bed. The event was scheduled for 10 a.m. the next morning and I was up bright and early for a good breakfast at eight o'clock... and out the door.

Who did I meet coming in only Galvin, Cooper and Donaghy. Cooper fell out of the cab first... Galvin next.. Donaghy after that, all of them the worse for wear from a night in Copper Face Jacks. And that's another thing about these Kerry boys that people in other counties might not understand. They can really enjoy themselves. When they party... it's flat out... one hundred per cent.

But when they train... *they train* and that is their sole focus. They can separate the two. And of course, when it comes to playing football, there is no group of footballers better in this country.

Different class.

They have been again today.

CHAPTER 26

David Heaney

And that's that.

The dream dies again.

But we were never really close. Sam stretched out his hand but we couldn't reach. It's like that scene you see in movies where a character is hanging out over a cliff... desperately hanging on to a person in danger of falling.

Slowly... slowly... slowly the grip loosens... and the person plunges to certain death. It's swift but ours is more drawn out... more public.

Cooper's scored three times but the problem is that one of them was a goal. Donaghy the same... Mike Frank with two points. And that's not as bad as people might think. If you're a defender... particularly in the full-back line... you're hoping to limit your man to a couple of scores.

Now if you can limit that across the six backs... that's 12 scores... maybe a 2-10 haul. You'd think that if you held Kerry to that, you'd be there or thereabouts. But the problem is that Kerry have had 10 different scorers today.

We had five.

I had three points but they were all frees... McDonald had a free...

Chuckie scored the two goals... Billy Joe popped over a point and Hartey scored a goal. Things could have been different if maybe Dillo got a couple... one from Ger Brady maybe, two from McGarrity perhaps. Another from Peadar... one from Higgins, which they were capable of.

That would have brought more respectability to the scoreline... but 3-5 is pitiful... especially as two of those goals came within a minute of each other.

I sit on the Croke Park pitch and wonder if I'll ever play in another All-Ireland final. Maybe I've had my shot.

Two of them!

We watch as Cooper and Declan O'Sullivan lift Sam Maguire into the skies. I'd rather be anywhere else right now but it's part of the tradition to wait... for the losers to wait around and watch the winners accept the silverware. That is one part of All-Ireland final pageantry that I don't mind.

You show respect to your opponents even after the final whistle has gone. I look around me... the lads are in bits.

We'd be better off out of here... now.

And we trudge off to the sound of Kerry cheering. I know this dressing room is going to be hard, particularly for the older lads.

This was their chance. And it's another All-Ireland final gone up in smoke closer to the end of a career. For the younger guys... there's some consolation in thinking that we'll be back here again.

And some day... surely... if we keep banging long enough, the door will open.

It has to.

David Heaney is another throwback to the mid 90s. Today is his third All-Ireland final defeat and, as team captain, this one will hit him particularly hard. He was full-back again, just as he was in 2004... and while the last two finals haven't gone particularly well for him it's unfair to heap too much criticism on the lad.

The fact that he was full back was a clear indication that we had no other player capable of playing better in that position. Brady came on and did well there today but Heaney is still more suited to the role.

The truth is that David is a monster of a footballer. He plays at midfield for us, full back, centre back… you can play him anywhere and be confident that he'll do a job.

He is a big figure in the dressing room and an inspirational speaker… when he does speak. An unassuming kind of guy, David doesn't speak just for the sake of it but when he has something to say, he is listened to. Much like Ciaran McDonald, when Heaney doesn't play… he is missed badly. There is nobody to fill the gap.

He doesn't really like the full back position and would prefer the freedom of the half back line or midfield but circumstances dictated that he was placed on the edge of the square.

Naturally, as he gets a bit older, the legs aren't what they used to be. Heaney's a *box to box* type of footballer. You see soccer players labelled as that… the guys who can get up and down the pitch but the difference in Gaelic football is that we're taking hits and have guys trying to mow us down as we embark on those lung-bursting runs.

It's different to soccer… there the belts and tackles aren't half as severe. That has taken it out of Heaney over the years, as it would with any player. Hence, he moved back the field and has been an effective full back, though I still would always prefer to see him at midfield.

Heaney understands his limitations as a footballer. He can kick a score but he is a forward's dream as a midfielder, instead preferring to take a second to look for a better placed team mate.

He is good craic too, on the training round and out for a couple of pints. He has his own crew and I often meet him in Galway for a jar. There is always a good chance that if Heaney is out, Maurice Sheridan will be too. And if Maurice is out, there is a fair chance that David Brady will be around the place. And if DB is, the chances are that Kenneth has his dancing shoes on.

It is a chain reaction. I like that about the guys who soldiered together in the 90s. They always stick together.

Successive managers have identified Heaney as a leader very quickly. And if there is a message that a manager wants to relay to a particular player,

Heaney is a good man to act as a conduit... arm around the shoulder and away you go.

He was really good to me last year, when I was dropped for the All-Ireland quarter-final defeat to Kerry. That was a frustrating time for me but that's when I really got to know Heaney.

He is always there to listen, which is great because he is a player I look up to. I always had Kenneth, Trevor and the rest of the family to talk to but Heaney is a member of the extended support group.

CHAPTER

Peadar Gardiner

The day began with a stark realisation, when the morning light flooded through the hotel bedroom curtains, and it will end with another. For the survivors from 1996 and '97, another All-Ireland final has passed them by without claiming the big prize. This may never happen for them.

And now they're a year closer to the end of their careers.

They're hurting more… they have to be. Tears are flowing but the players that have been here two years ago know how to handle them. It's more embarrassment than raw hurt that I'm feeling but there's nothing that we can do about it now. We had our chance and it passed us by again.

Some of the younger lads are wondering where we're going for a pint…what are the post match arrangements?

I can't remember if Jack O'Connor has come into out dressing room to commiserate. I'm in a daze. Moran and Morrison are much the same.

Shell-shocked.

We shower and sit down, pulling on our clothes, fumbling through gear bags… it's the only thing to do to keep occupied. Better that than talk to someone.

Nobody is talking anyway.

Moran and Morrison break the silence with a few short words. They thank us for our efforts. It's soon decided that there won't be a homecoming in Mayo tomorrow night. It's too f*****g embarrassing.

An exchange of views on the matter leads to the decision that it won't be happening. I would have thought it more respectful to greet the supporters at home, even if it was p*****g down with rain. After all, they've been with us all year and paid good money to watch the team play. Surely it's the least they deserve but I can understand why it's not happening.

We head for the players' bar in the stadium... the Kerry lads are already tucking into a couple of well-earned bottles. After a while, I notice that our County Board chairman, James Waldron is sitting with Moran and Morrison.

I wander over... the feeling is that the lads will get a second year.

I'd heard talk about John O'Mahony previously and that heaped a bit of pressure on Mickey and John, I felt. It was unfair too because they're good guys and they've had me in the form of my life this season.

'Yeah, yeah... they'll definitely get another chance,' Waldron tells me.

Mickey and John had refused to take a training session before the Laois quarter-final, because of the amount of club games at senior and Under-21 level. There was some speculation floating about that they might even quit but they returned after meeting with Waldron.

I've read too from others in the county that Moran and Morrison weren't training us hard enough but, hand on heart... this doesn't add up for me. A lot of the stuff we did in training was tactical, and the guys needed to be doing their own bit outside of training.

Were we being trained hard enough?

Let me put it this way, we've only lost one Championship game all year and that was the All-Ireland final. We came through a replay against Laois and we were going really strong at the end of the Dublin game.

Draw your own conclusions.

I decide not to head straight back to the Citywest Hotel after the game... I need some time on my own. So I go to nearby Saggart for a few drinks before linking up with the rest of the lads back at the hotel.

As the night progresses, spirits lift.

It's like that.

Everyone gets a few beers down their necks and the positivity returns, even as we're at our lowest. But deep down I know that Monday's coming.

And that's hard.

Dying from drink… and dying inside after what's happened the day before. And it's everywhere again… papers, TV and radio. There's no homecoming so I decide to stay in Dublin for the day… go on the beer again.

Right now, there's still an aching pain that has to be numbed.

I know there's a fair chance Trevor will be drowning his sorrows with Peadar Gardiner. But if Peadar is having a few beers, he knows when to cap the night. He's sensible like that and he is best friends with Trevor for a number of years. They lived together in Tuam and Peadar is a member of our dressing room circle.

He didn't deserve this… none of us did.

It was an almost pitiful sight watching Peadar dragging himself to the touchline when he went off injured in the second half.

Broken body… broken spirit.

Peadar's from Crossmolina, and is one of life's good guys. He isn't an extrovert by any means… a normal chap, and a real pillar of his local community.

Peadar's club form is always exceptional with Crossmolina and… he is just a fabulous club player and clubman. He never misses training and usually plays well in big games for Cross'.

I've often thought that if I played for another county, I would be the type of person that Peadar would think was a f****** eejit… with some of my carry-on. Peadar is more normal and he likes things to be as such.

When somebody goes beyond normal, he wonders what they are doing? He must have often wondered what he let himself in for… with both McDonald and myself on the panel. But Peadar is used to McDonald… they play for the same club, and as time has progressed we've had more and more time for one another too.

My parents loved watching him play, granddad George too. It was that marauding style, up and down the wing, that really caught the eye.

Peadar works hard at training and when he does go for a few pints, he is good craic. But if I'm on a night out, I'll say, 'Let's keep going hard.'

And if someone else says we'll go hard, I'll say we should go harder. Peadar, however, knows his cut-off points… his limits. You'll never see him falling out the door of a pub or nightclub. He is smart and never finds himself in a situation where he could be embarrassed.

As a footballer, he never complains on the training pitch and the long runs don't bother him. Peadar… like me… knows it is simply a case that Kerry were too good for us. No excuses. They were the better side with the better players and the gulf in class was so big that if Kerry played badly, they could still have won the All-Ireland final.

It's like this… if I'm playing against you and I'm a better player, I'm going to beat you. And that will manifest itself on a wider scale if the opposition are better players in 10 or 12 positions, which is the case with Kerry.

When that's the case, of course they're going to win the game. The better team won't win by 14 points all of the time but they should still get over the line. I know that and Peadar's deeply analytical mind understands it too.

I was never a fan of some people in the Mayo County Board. I have always wondered why they are in their jobs in the first place. They're the people that you have to go to for a ticket for the match. And they know that. They thrive on it.

I don't know for sure how they will treat Mickey Moran and John Morrison. I have spoken to both men and told them that I was privileged and honoured to have worked with them.

Naturally, both men are disappointed.

And they want to do more with us as a group.

Mickey and John didn't get us over the line and that's a pity. They are honest, gave their all and wanted players to improve. They talked big when they took over the team, about Connacht titles and All-Irelands.

But their primary goal was to ensure that a player was better when they left. That's the proper attitude to have as a coach or manager. And if you can improve players who are good already, you will win things.

That goes for Mayo the same as any other county.

Surely?

PART THREE
In The End

CHAPTER 28

Pain has continued to be a constant companion of Mayo football since 2006. We lost two more All-Ireland finals in 2012 and 2013, and in 2014 we watched another manager, James Horan slip by without landing the big prize.

County board officials came under fire, once again, for their handling of the appointment process after Horan's exit which has seen Noel Connelly and Pat Holmes installed as joint managers.

So, what about some of the others? Billy Joe declared for Armagh and I felt he got a raw deal there too. He decided to retire from county football before the 2013 season, when the Armagh manager Paul Grimley left him out of his panel. I'm not privy to what went on there and Billy Joe publicly stated that he had no axe to grind with Grimley but I've seen plenty of Armagh forwards play and they wouldn't be capable of feeding their leading forward Jamie Clarke like Billy Joe can.

Moran and Morrison?
There's another story.

They were pushed aside after the 2006 final but they're still involved in the game, as they should be. Mickey and John went on to manage Leitrim but John encountered ill-health before returning to the game as manager of the Monaghan ladies senior team. Mickey claimed another notable success with University of Ulster, Jordanstown, helping to guide them to victory in the 2008 Sigerson Cup. The old saying rings true for me in that regard. Form is temporary but class is permanent.

That's certainly the case with Mickey.

I'm still in touch with Austin O'Malley and he's as fit as ever. The six-pack is still there and Austy kept on going, kept on fighting. He kicked a massive winning point against Kerry in the National League in 2008. We were level with them when I had a late chance that I put wide. But Austy stepped up to nail the winner.

I'll always remember Austy for those five points against Kerry, and Marc Ó Sé, in that 2005 quarter-final. I envied that, looking on from the bench. And against Ó Sé! The one man I always wanted to go toe to toe with! But the breaks didn't fall often enough for Austy and when John O'Mahony took over, Austy flitted in and out again.

O'Mahony named his squad for the 2010 Championship and Austy was cut. He later transferred to Wicklow and won a Division 4 title with them in 2012, before returning home to Louisburgh.

As for Dillo, he's still doing what he does best, playing senior football for Mayo and striving for Sam.

Travelling and spending some time with this man in Thailand, Australia, New Zealand and South Africa was something else. A total of €2,500 each, I think it cost us in November of 2009... all flights to all destinations included in that. It was a trip that kicked off with a bang when we blew most of our budget over the course of two wild nights in Singapore.

Not surprising considering that a shot of vodka there was €28 a pop. Thailand was incredible, the highlight being the Koh Phangan full moon party with thousands of people on the beach. We were fleeced by pickpockets before we got back to the mainland, and sea sick all the way over.

We stayed in chalets in Ko Samui, and had another beach party on Phi Phi Island, visiting "The Beach" where the movie of the same name starring Leonardo DiCaprio was filmed, and got seasick again.

We watched Thai boxing matches, and drank through straws from buckets full to the brim with ice and alcohol. We had a trip to Pattaya city and the gogo bars there. It was a different world... pool parties in Phuket. Two young lads living the dream and escaping from football for a while.

Nights in Perth drifted away over a few cool bottles of Corona... Cairns... Brisbane, white water rafting and pushing Dillo into one of the rapids! We met the former Liverpool striker, Robbie Fowler in Queensland, and I got my picture taken with one of my all-time heroes. We bought a car for 50 bucks from a guy in Cairns, no tax or insurance... and the fear in the pair of us when the electrics failed and the lights went out driving through the Bush in the dark of night! We drove the 1,700km from Cairns to Brisbane, visited Fraser Island, partied in random towns, took on board warnings not to swim in shark-infested lakes and also to beware of the wild dingoes on our various stops.

We spent time in Sydney and found out the next day that Adam Scott, the champion Aussie golfer, had been refused entry to the Mercantile Hotel on The Rocks on the same night that we were in there. On New Year's Eve we were watching the fireworks over Sydney Harbour, and meeting random Mayo people from Castlebar and Breaffy.

One day Dillo wanted to visit Bondi Beach and I let him at it because that area was too much like home... full of Irish and yet I still ended up drinking for the day with an Irish backpacker named Barry. I was sitting outside a pub and this guy walked past with an Ireland jersey, photographing everything that he possibly could as he strolled. We went on the booze for the day and Barry lost his camera, backpack... the lot.

Dillo and I went on to New Zealand, to Queenstown and Hastings, where my uncle lived – on the North Island on the way to Auckland. We stayed there for a week and had the house to ourselves. It was a time to draw breath, relax, and get some good food in.

Uncle Austin, a fitness fanatic, had a stationary exercise bike at the back of the house and when he worked out, he'd put on a video of Lance Armstrong shouting at him and motivating him. I wonder what Austin thinks of the fallen star now?

We watched the former All Black, Joe Rokocoko strutting his stuff in the Super 15, and visited the fantastic Crusaders' Stadium in Christchurch. From New Zealand we headed to South Africa. We struggled to find a place to stay before finally we stumbled on a unique B & B where the owner had a swimming pool and a garage with kegs and beer taps. At the time, South Africa was gearing up for the World Cup in 2010 and we visited the stadium in Durban and watched the Orlando Pirates playing nearby. There was more rugby as we watched the famous Sharks going through their paces at their training base. We had our pictures taken with John Smit, the former Springbok player and the Beast, Tendai Mtawarira.

Our lives flashed before our eyes on a night out when we were the only white people in a nightclub.

'Come downstairs… and I'll show you around,' one guy said to us.

This is it, I thought to myself, …*all over!*

What lay beneath was amazing.

A cigar room… poker room… whiskey room. After that night on the tiles, the early house beckoned and I asked for a beer. Dillo was hungry and being the healthy type that he is, he went for the muesli option.

I was low on cash and headed for the nearest ATM. Two hours later, Dillo was hovering over me. I'd fallen asleep under the ATM.

Fleeced again.

Wallet gone.

A low point.

From Durban we headed to Cape Town, where we trained hard. And then to Port Elizabeth, where I had relations there, Loretta and Bill. It was a 15-hour bus trip to get there but, again, we trained hard because home and a return to the Mayo squad was within our sights. A short stop in Johannesburg followed and then it was time for home… for sure.

Back to reality.

***

Back to the hard graft.

But those weeks with Dillo were unforgettable and that trip was life-changing in many ways. It opened my eyes to new people, new cultures... new ways of living. And it reminded me of just how good it can be to get away from Ireland for a while, even if it was only for a relatively short time.

Some of those nights out were euphoric but in my entire life, there's one that will always stand out above all others. Winning a Sigerson Cup medal with Dublin City University was special in its own right as I was directly involved but it's not often that you get to witness a sporting miracle unfold in front of your very eyes. I was one of the 69,000 people packed into the Atatürk Stadium in Istanbul on May 25, 2005, when my beloved Liverpool came from 0-3 down to win the European Cup against AC Milan.

I picked up one of the last package deals available from 747 Travel in Dublin and managed to source three tickets for the game from Frankie Dolan in Roscommon, who had good contacts. It's amazing when I think back on it now that I arrived home with two of those tickets unused. I assumed that I'd have no trouble getting rid of them.

The night before the game, I wandered into a bar, which was pretty much empty until a group of women walked in. They were the wives and girlfriends of the Liverpool players and I remember talking to Harry Kewell's wife, the actress Sheree Murphy at the bar. Steven Gerrard's wife, Alex was there too and meeting them wasn't a bad way to kick off the trip!

I managed to get some inside information on the team that would be picked the following night and if I'd phoned home, I could have got some of my friends to put money on the starting line-up.

The match itself was nothing short of sensational. The Atatürk was a fair bit out of town and it was almost like a pilgrimage as thousands of fans walked a couple of miles to the stadium. It was a tense atmosphere because the Turks don't particularly like English people. And if you were wearing a Liverpool shirt that night, you were cast as an Englishman.

I was glad when we arrived... the banter outside the stadium was electric. I was on my own but I didn't care and I got in nice and early, two hours before kick-off. By half-time the game looked over as AC Milan led 3-0 but Liverpool launched the fight back in the second half.

Gerrard 1-3… Vladimir Smicer 2-3… Xabi Alonso 3-3.

Extra-time… penalties and glory.

It was a feeling that I cannot describe. I remember ringing people at home after the game in a state of absolute elation. Even if I won an All-Ireland title with Mayo, I don't know if that feeling would even compare. This was something else. This was Liverpool, the team I had supported all of my life winning the biggest prize in club soccer. The celebrations were incredible as Liverpool supporters soaked it up in Taksim Square.

Two years later, Liverpool were within touching distance of the prize again, when they played AC Milan once more in the final, this time in Athens. I travelled over with Trevor from Dublin, via Liverpool. It was a nighmarish trip in some respects. Security outside the Olympic Stadium was dreadful and fans with genuine tickets were denied access.

Kenneth was also there but he bought a dud and couldn't get in. Twenty minutes before kick-off, Trevor and I paid €1,000 each for two tickets but it was still mayhem at the gates outside. We managed to get through the first security check but there was still a walk ahead of us before we got to the stadium itself. Me and Trevor were dodging past security men and in the stampede we were forced to run over a gate that had fallen, with other supporters stuck underneath it. It was horrible.

Trevor and I wouldn't be the huggy-huggy types but when we got inside the gate, which meant that we were definitely getting into the game… we hugged. It was sheer relief. The game didn't pan out as we would have wanted as AC Milan won 2-1. Liverpool played better than in 2005… and I'd seen them in two finals. One win… one defeat.

Not a bad record. Certainly one I'd have taken from those two All-Ireland finals with Mayo.

***

That trip to Athens was slap bang in the middle of the Championship season. Mickey Moran and John Morrison were gone. We had a new team boss. The treatment of Moran and Morrison disappointed me. I had spoken to both men after they left and told them how much I had enjoyed working with them.

'Look,' I told them, 'What do you expect from the guys that you're dealing with?'

Naturally, both men were disappointed at how it all ended. And you don't normally sign a deal to manage a county team for a year; it's normally two or three. I felt embarrassed by the actions of our County Board… the Board that is supposed to represent our team. Here we were, airing our dirty linen in public yet again.

It was a disgrace. Two men that had taken us to an All-Ireland final were gone a month later. It still annoys me to this day but nothing surprises me with the County Board.

When I won an All Star award at the end of 2006, I texted Mickey and John and thanked them both. They had improved me as a footballer and they were good coaches. You'll sometimes find that a team is knocking on the door for a few years and suddenly a manager comes in and they win the Championship.

I'd love to know what the County Board's reasons were for getting rid of Moran and Morrison. It couldn't be because we were beaten in an All-Ireland final because when they took over, there was nothing expected of us. And that leads me to the biggest problem of all in Mayo… supporters and clubs don't hold the County Board accountable enough.

So the question I'd ask is this: Why were Mickey Moran and John Morrison shafted? Following on from that… why was there no document explaining the reasons why?

With the departure of Moran and Morrison, the guessing game began as players and supporters wondered who would step in? There was one name on everybody's lips… a man viewed as a messiah. He had been in charge when Mayo contested the 1989 All-Ireland final and he managed Galway to two All-Ireland victories in 1998 and 2001.

He was a Mayo man and the word on the street was that he had unfinished business to attend to. We'd come so close to the Holy Grail and there was one man that could finally take us across the finishing line.

That man was John O'Mahony.

CHAPTER 29

IT was one of those crazy days that often follows a crazy night.

I'd been out all night and ended up attending a house party back at the Dublin City University campus.

It was during the 2009 National Football League, I was out of action with a wrist injury sustained against Tyrone and in the mood for a blow out. When football was in full swing, I'd rarely venture out and I certainly wasn't as lively on the social scene as I was during my first year at DCU.

The next morning, the only pub open in the local area was Matt Weldon's, formerly The Slipper, located across the road from the DCU entrance on the Glasnevin Road.

I was in there with Meath's Kevin Reilly and a few of his mates for a couple of early morning pints.

Stepping outside for a breath of fresh air, a grey Laguna car pulled up outside the pub. Kevin turned to me.

'They're here for me,' he told me quickly.

Kevin, it seems, had passed a smart remark to a local girl in one of the nearby shops, some comment about the pyjamas she had been wearing. Not very wise at the time I guess, but Kevin had a few on board.

Sure enough, a few lads jumped out of the Laguna and went for Kevin. I jumped in to help him out but slipped on the path, landed on my elbow and popped my shoulder.

The incident was over in seconds and the guys in the Laguna drove away. Over one of the nearby doors, I noticed a sign for a surgery.

I banged on the door and pleaded for my shoulder to be put back into place. I was informed that it was a veterinary clinic, and neither was the person who opened the door best pleased.

Shane Roche from Wexford drove me to Beaumont Hospital and, at that stage, I was in considerable discomfort. I was sitting in the passenger seat, trying to hold my elbow steady in an attempt to keep the shoulder solid. The pain was excruciating and very soon the other unfortunate souls in the Accident and Emergency Department knew all about it.

There was a big queue when I arrived but I made my way to the front desk and demanded to be seen. I was urged to sit down by the attendant but instead, I scuttled in around the back of the A & E, pushed through the emergency doors, sat down on a chair and roared for help.

When I came to, things were better.

I'd obviously been sedated before my shoulder was popped back into place. In town a while later, I met one of the workers in Beaumont who was on duty that morning.

'Do you remember me?' he enquired. 'I was working in the A & E on the morning that you were brought in.'

It was embarrassing. I couldn't remember who he was.

I arrived back to DCU later in the day, tail between my legs after my hospital experience. I checked my phone and it was red hot, with John O'Mahony among the callers and texters.

I tried to blot the world out by pulling the blinds in my apartment but sleep didn't come easily. I knew I'd have to face the music. O'Mahony had left voice messages, asking me to ring him urgently. He heard that something had happened and the fear rose to my throat as I wondered exactly what I would tell him.

Eventually, I plucked up the courage to ring John.

'I hear that you're after breaking your shoulder,' he stated.

'I hurt it alright,' I replied, '… slipped outside playing soccer.'

I'm sure he didn't buy my story and I presume it was a tale that John stored in the memory bank. Journalists were also trying to contact me. Word had travelled fast.

I had nothing to say.

Nothing had happened.

That was my stance.

Five or six weeks later, I returned to training with Mayo.

I was back when the cast came off my hand and the timelines with the shoulder injury coincided with each other. So I felt that I could mask the shoulder problem pretty well, make out that it wasn't as bad as it was - and that the episode that caused it wasn't that bad either. But I was only fooling myself.

And I certainly wasn't fooling O'Mahony.

The shoulder was tender for the remainder of the season. I was told that I didn't need an operation but that I'd have to work on it. When you dislocate your shoulder, as I had, a protective fibrous cap is torn and never recovers. That's why some players suffer repeated dislocations of the joint. Damage it once, and there's a fair chance you'll do it again.

But I was in the gym building it back up… sometimes twice a day with weights.

I had four weeks of good training before the Championship opener against Roscommon. But when the team was announced, I wasn't in it.

We ran up a big score and I felt that John had held the shoulder episode against me. I was probably naïve to assume that he didn't know the full story – very soon after "Reilly-gate" it seemed that everybody knew exactly what had happened the pair of us.

My cause wasn't helped either by missing out on League football and challenge games before the Championship. I'd got the vibe in a trial game the week before too.

I played on the "B" team and that was normally a good indicator of where a player stood. Aidan Kilcoyne, who was picked ahead of me, Pat Harte from a penalty, and Aidan O'Shea scored the goals as we ran out big winners. I was pleased for "Killer", a good player who had been doing well at club level for Knockmore.

I looked on helplessly from the dugout as the lads romped to a 3-17 to 0-7 win. It was a turkey shoot. We were 3-10 to 0-1 ahead at half-time. Trevor scored a couple of points… Dillon got six. After the game, I was experiencing bittersweet emotions. I was delighted the lads had done so well but, on that evidence before me, there was no way back into the team for the Connacht final against Galway.

Nevertheless, I put the head down and trained hard for the next four weeks. I continued to hold out hope of a starting place but O'Mahony told me that I'd be coming on and I was happy enough with that.

I was sprung from the bench at half-time.

Michael Jackson's death captured the attention of music lovers all over the world. Even if you didn't like the King of Pop's brand of music, you couldn't help but be fascinated by his life, which was bizarre on so many levels.

I had some spare time on my hands that summer. I had no work and I was watching the fallout from Jackson's death and his subsequent funeral on Sky News. It was practically wall-to-wall coverage and I was hooked. I couldn't get enough of it.

I guess I was in my own kind of crazy routine. Struggling to occupy my time and my mind, Jackson's death filled a void. There were the stories about his life, what he was like as a person, his troubles, and the abuse cases against him. I felt sympathy for the guy and, in addition… I'd always liked his music.

To this day, I still do.

As well as that, I'd always liked soccer players who had an extravagant streak, especially when it came to goal celebrations. I'd already received a pair of customised boots from Adidas, who were sponsoring me at the time, with the words "MJ Mort" inscribed on them. I tipped off a journalist that I would be wearing them at Pearse Stadium and the journalist informed a photographer from the Inpho sports agency, who was prepped on what to expect.

The decision to don a t-shirt in Jackson's honour came later in the week. On the eve of the game in fact. I was sitting at home on the Saturday night, struggling to while away the time, as usual, when the thought struck me.

Yeah, I'll get on tomorrow, I was thinking.

And when I do I'm going to surprise a few people.

I sourced a plain white t-shirt from my wardrobe and got to work. I scrawled the words "RIP Micheal Jackson" on the front, tucked in into my gear bag and smiled to myself as I pictured what it might be like to pull my Mayo jersey over my head to reveal what lay beneath.

Getting the t-shirt on in the dressing room before the game would prove more difficult than I could have imagined.

I was looking around, desperately hoping that nobody would see what I was doing. I had the t-shirt half on me, settled on my shoulders, before pulling on my Mayo jersey.

With it now safely concealed, I could reach underneath and innocently pull the t-shirt down over my torso. I was turned into the corner so that nobody could see what I was doing.

I read later that in sporting careers some of the best and craziest stories are the ones that you simply can't make up. Sure enough, with eight minutes remaining, my chance arrived.

Trevor did brilliantly to get past Finian Hanley to create a two-on-one situation. The pass put an open goal on a plate for me and we were seven points clear.

When the ball hit the net, I forgot that I had the t-shirt on.

I was simply lost in the moment.

Scoring a goal creates a phenomenal, indescribable rush. It can last for a 20 seconds... half a minute... longer.

I lifted my Mayo shirt to display my special message to Michael Jackson. Job done and back into the game again.

With time running out, Ronan McGarrity and I decided to play some keep-ball in an attempt to wind down the clock. We coughed up possession and Michael Meehan shrugged off Ger Cafferkey before finding the back of the net. Galway, incredibly, were level but there was still time for one last twist as Andy Moran spotted Peadar Gardiner running into space. Peadar split the posts and we were home…with just a point to spare.

The post-match headlines should have been about Peadar and his superb winner but it wasn't long before attention was focused on my t-shirt… and my poor spelling.

I didn't realise that I had written the name Michael as Micheal. Maybe I tried spelling it in Irish!

If I did, I certainly forgot the *fada*. I haven't seen that t-shirt since, incidentally. I left it back in my bag when I went for a shower after the game. It was two days before I realised that it was gone, when I went to empty my smelly bag. I suspect that our kit man, Noel Howley or Pat Harte was the culprit.

To this day, I've never gotten to the bottom of it but the knowing smiles on Noel's and Pat's faces when I've quizzed them about the missing t-shirt do nothing to quell my suspicion!

I decided to get away to Manchester that night.

A wise move, perhaps, as I'd been arrested on a previous night out in Galway.

But it wasn't long before I gathered that John O'Mahony was unimpressed by my tribute to Jackson. He spoke to me at length when we returned to training a few days later.

'Why did you do it?'

He must have asked me that question 10 times.

'You took away from the victory…

'… you took away from Peadar's point… it's all about you…

'…it's always all about you… you in the paper again.'

He was furious.

O'Mahony mentioned that Trevor Howley's grandmother had died on the Saturday night and that I should have been more respectful. I genuinely didn't know that Trevor and his family had suffered a bereavement.

I stressed to John that the jersey stunt was merely a bit of craic. I imagined my team mates felt the same about it.

Some of them perhaps… maybe not all of them.

We went out of the 2009 Championship against Meath in the All-Ireland quarter-final. I didn't start the game and perhaps that had something to do with the jersey episode. I'm not sure but I was surprised not to get the start. We lost by 1-15 to 2-15 at Croke Park and I came on at half-time, and scored four points after replacing Tom Parsons.

I should have known better than to lie to O'Mahony because I'd been caught out before. I don't know how he managed it but he just knew if you'd stepped out of line. He always knew.

I still enjoyed a great relationship with him. If you were honest and truthful with Johno, you'd have no problems. But if you told lies, it was bad news. He wouldn't be happy with that. And the lies that people told were silly lies, like not training and telling him that you were going here and there.

I was crushed when he told us that he was leaving after the 2010 All-Ireland qualifier defeat against Longford. He'd been there for four seasons and a reign that began with such hope finished on a bum note after a shocking display from us. As players, we'd let him down.

I shed a tear and wished him well. When he took over the job from Mickey Moran and John Morrison, the county was awash with hope. It was the second coming and Johno had done it for Galway! Why not Mayo?

Surely now it was our time.

I'd worked with Johno previously at interprovincial level with Connacht. The bottom line is that during his time with Mayo, we didn't get the best out of ourselves to match what he was giving us in return. We won that Connacht title in 2009 but our relative lack of success during his four seasons was down to us as players.

When we crossed the line, it was nothing to do with Johno. He could not have prepared us better. Everything about him was meticulous – the food, the hotels we stayed in, the emphasis on hydration. It was much more than that. It was a thousand things.

He did most of the talking in the papers coming up to the big games and that took pressure off players. And during his time as manager of Galway, I had learned that he posted an interview that I had done before the game against them on their dressing room wall.

It was a Connacht final and Galway beat us. I was talking s**** about Galway, obviously, and it was a good lesson for me to learn going forward.

O'Mahony trusted players but he demanded our trust too. If he didn't get it, he was quick to find out why?

Before one Tuesday evening training session, I told Johno that I had an exam in college. In fact, I was off to Marbella for a few days with an ex of mine. I wasn't missing anything major at the time but Johno always marked off participation at training.

'Conor Mortimer is doing exams… but we're checking that out,' he told the rest of the group.

Dillo texted me to tip me off and I knew that something was up. When I arrived back into Dublin, my flight was delayed.

I had to be at training the same evening.

Johno demanded that I meet him in his office in Claremorris.

'Conor… come in, sit down. How are things?'

'Fine, John.'

'Tell me… where were you?'

The game was up. I debated for a couple of seconds about whether or not I should keep up the pretence but there was no point in dragging it out. The game was well and truly up.

'I was away with herself in Marbella.'

I felt like a right p***k.

There was silence for a few moments.

'Look… why didn't you tell me?'

I told Johno that I didn't feel that he was approachable and at the time, I really felt and meant that. Maybe it had something to do with his aura. John was such a dominant figure, now involved in the world of politics, and he carried a huge presence.

'Look, John… it was my mistake. I shouldn't have done it.'

Once I'd held my hands up and admitted that I was wrong, Johno had no problem with that. If a player is honest with him, he'll be fine but try to dodge bullets and he'll be in trouble.

Some time later, we were on a training weekend in Kildare and left to our own devices. A group exercise was arranged, in an open forum format where if a player wanted to say or share something, the floor was his.

David Brady stood up.

'I told O'Mahony that you were away on holidays,' said Brady.

'You p***k!' I blurted.

I couldn't believe it.

DB… of all people? The same fella could be away himself on a regular basis! After a good chuckle, all was well with the world again.

The 2009 Connacht final win was the highlight of Johno's tenure but there should have been more, much more. And his appointment had helped in some ways to calm the anger that was brewing inside me after the way Mickey Moran and John Morrison had been treated by the County Board after the 2006 final. Surely it should have been about keeping some continuity and building on what we had achieved the previous year?

Not with this County Board, obviously. But O'Mahony had been linked with the job before and he was portrayed as a messianic figure in Mayo. The missing link, the man who could finally tie it all together and turn us into All-Ireland champions for the first time since 1951.

I'd heard good things about O'Mahony from his time with Galway. But the thing about that Galway team – and Pádraic Joyce has told me this - is that they should have won more All-Irelands. They had incredible players like Joyce, Derek Savage, Michael Donnellan, Tomás Mannion, Seán Óg de Paor, Tomás Meehan and Deccie Meehan. And I used to watch them almost every week. I hardly missed a game they played on their way to glory in 1998.

O'Mahony was *the big reason* why they won those two All-Irelands. And if any of the players had personal issues, he'd try and sort something out for them. But as a Mayo man, O'Mahony's heart was with his native county. It felt to me like the entire county of Mayo believed that with O'Mahony in charge, all we had to do was flick a switch and... hey presto, we would become All-Ireland champions. That was pressure right from the start but O'Mahony had huge confidence in his managerial abilities and his track record spoke for itself.

In a footballing sense, we never got going while he was in charge. We got stale after 2006 and it's very difficult for a manager to arrest that. And I don't think that he had a high enough quality of back-up in his management team to help him through.

There was also a criticism of Johno at the time that his developing career in politics impacted on the Mayo job. It's not something that I paid too much heed to. There was an odd night when he wasn't there, not enough to upset a team but when Johno wasn't there, he was missed.

Kieran Gallagher was kept on from the previous regime and I didn't agree with that. No disrespect to Kieran but when a management team is sacked or let go, the whole team should go, not just one or two. You expect a clean sweep and I would have preferred if a former player came on board with Johno.

He brought in Tommy Lyons, a good guy with his heart in Mayo football, and Peter Burke was the goalkeeping coach. But Johno needed more than that. You look around at the top teams now and the skill sets are so high. Managers surround themselves with proven quality and proven winners. Sports science and strength and conditioning has evolved to such a high level and the skill sets of these practitioners are so high. You won't get a job at club level if you're not up to scratch, never mind county level. But this lack of quality assistance wasn't Johno's fault.

He was top notch but busy too in his own job. It's an amateur game after all and he wasn't getting paid to manage Mayo. His day-to-day job was politics and while I'm sure he found it difficult to balance the two, he gave Mayo everything he could.

***

O'Mahony's management style was player-friendly but my experiences proved that it was difficult to get away with much. Pat Harte was another who got caught out. Hartey travelled a lot with work and while he was home one evening, he obviously wasn't in the form for training. He rang Johno and told him that he was still abroad.

But as he drove out of Ballaghaderreen on this particular evening, who did he overtake in the car only O'Mahony! I don't know if the pair of them ever spoke about that, or if Johno copped on that it was Hartey, but Pat was straight on the phone to me.

'You'll never guess who I'm after passing out!'

One of my biggest regrets is that we didn't win an All-Ireland under O'Mahony. In Johno's final year in charge, the warning signs were there in Connacht when we lost to Sligo by 1-8 to 0-15. I had a good first half in that game but I messed with my boots at half-time and I couldn't kick snow off a rope in the second half. To finish the year losing against Longford at Pearse Park was low. Johno deserved better than that.

We lost by a point but it was a shocking way to end.

In that Pearse Park dressing room, he told us that his time was up, that he'd given us what he could. I gave him a hug and he could see that I was upset. I felt close to Johno – when I came back from Australia earlier in the year, Johno gave me a lift home from Dublin. There wasn't much chat mind you, because from the minute I sat into the car his phone was ringing constantly.

I've spoken to Johno a few times since.

I met him at Michaela Harte's funeral in January 2011, and I ring him now and then, just to check in and enquire about how he's doing?

I'm still in awe of John O'Mahony. In his presence, it's like talking to the President. I still wonder what I should say to the man and when I do splutter out a few words, I'm left thinking if I've said the right thing at all?

Johno also made Trevor captain of Mayo during his time in charge and that was a gesture deeply appreciated by our family. But, ultimately, another man that came in labelled as Mayo's messiah had found the quest for the

Holy Grail too big an ask.

And so the responsibility was passed on to the next incumbent.

This man was familiar to me, a former teammate and a forward of some renown during his playing days. And having guided Ballintubber to the 2010 Mayo county title after defeating Castlebar Mitchels, James Horan saw off the challenges of Tommy Lyons and Anthony McGarry to become the county's new senior football team manager.

CHAPTER 30

THE former Dublin player Mark Vaughan accidentally smashed my nose in January 2009. I was playing for Dublin City University against Dublin IT in an O'Byrne Cup quarter-final and while this might have been just one of those regular pre-season matches, there was still plenty at stake.

As DCU players, DIT were big city rivals of ours at the time. Throw in the fact that I was from Mayo and Vaughan played for the Dubs and there was always the potential for a flashpoint. Mark landed on me with his two knees into the back of my head as I lay face down in the mud after collecting the ball. It wasn't a particularly nice thing to happen but I know that he didn't go out deliberately to break my nose.

I got straight up and drew a boot across him but missed. My nose was sprayed across the right side of my face, with blood pouring from it.

But after some patch up work, I still managed to come away with six points and we won by 0-11 to 0-5. I never held it against Vaughan, who I got to know on a personal level in recent years. He was renowned as something of a wild child and while Mark had the capacity to kick some fine long-range scores, his natural skills weren't what they could have been. He played a lot of rugby when he was younger and it was only in later years that he began to develop as a Gaelic footballer.

A broken nose was child's play compared to the most serious injury of my career. In April 2001, Mayo were crowned Connacht Under-21 football champions for the first time in four years but on a misty evening in Castlebar, disaster struck.

I'd been doing well on my marker, Sligo's Patrick Naughton. I had a couple of points on the board and moved to collect a ball angled towards the touchline, as Mayo attacked the Albany End of McHale Park.

I fired a pass with the outside of my left boot but Naughton came in to block down the ball and came down on my knee. I connected with Naughton's leg on the follow through and within a couple of seconds, I was crumpled in a heap on the greasy sod.

The pain was excruciating, unlike anything that I had ever experienced before. Describing it is tricky... it was like putting a bomb in the middle of my knee and then pressing a button to detonate it. I was down for a few minutes and when I got up, I was little more than a passenger, hobbling around. At half-time, I was insistent that I was not coming off and after my knee was strapped, I reappeared for the second half.

I managed to score two further points before going off but they were scores kicked with a straight left leg. When a player kicks a score, the knee is usually bent but I couldn't bend it. It was out like a balloon, swollen and heavily bandaged.

The big problem was that nobody sent me for a scan to ascertain the exact nature of the injury. I missed the All-Ireland semi-final victory over Meath but there was plenty of time to get right for the final, which wasn't played until October because of the Foot and Mouth crisis.

But I couldn't walk for two months after damaging my knee. I was sitting at home on the couch with the leg up and I couldn't work for Dad either. I iced my knee every day, thinking that it was getting better.

In that final against Tyrone, I scored four points but I couldn't twist or turn. My knee was so weak. We lost by three points but that was no disgrace because Tyrone were a serious team at the time. They had players like Conor Gormley, Philip Jordan, Ryan Mellon, Brian McGuigan, Stephen O'Neill, Enda McGinley, Kevin Hughes, Owen Mulligan and the late, great Cormac McAnallen. Those guys would go on to form the core of the team that made the All-Ireland senior breakthrough in 2003.

I continued to play in spite of the injury, not knowing the full extent of the problem. There were a couple of times when, if the ground was hard and it had rained, the knee would buckle from underneath me if I received the ball in the corner and went to turn hard. It might sound funny but no defender seemed to cop onto that for 10 years. On one occasion my knee gave way and I just stood there, dropped the ball and presented it to the guy who was marking me.

When I stopped for a few moments, whatever had displaced would pop back into position again and I'd crack on.

Two years passed before James O'Toole, a physio in Galway, voiced his suspicions that I had cruciate ligament damage. But I'd read that the Armagh player, Kieran McGeeney, and some top NFL players in America had played on despite suffering cruciate injuries. Surely I could do the same? I embarked on a course of heavy weights. McGeeney, for example, had built up his quads and hamstrings to cope with dynamic movements, rather than opting for surgery.

But my knee was continuing to annoy me and if I turned sharply, it would sometimes give way underneath me completely. I could almost feel the bones rubbing off each other, with a definite *clicking* sound. Biting the bullet, I visited Ray Moran, a top surgeon in Dublin and after running a few tests Ray confirmed that my cruciate was gone.

'Go out there and get a date for your surgery,' Ray urged me. He didn't see me again for eight years.

When I did eventually return, in February 2011, Ray told me that I had amazed him, playing for so long without cruciate ligaments in my left knee. Sure, the injury had affected me but not enough to hinder my playing career. And because the recovery period for an injury of that nature was so long, I didn't want to risk missing a year of football. By now, James Horan had taken charge of the Mayo senior football team. I was anxious to make an impression and the prospect of surgery on my left knee was not ideal.

Unfortunately, I was left with no choice.

Training at Jordanstown's indoor facility shortly before Christmas, I ran the length of the pitch with the ball before, checking back, I turned heavily on that left knee. An opponent came in from the side, hit my knee and pushed it inwards. That pain again. That old, familiar pain that I had first experienced back in 2001. This time, the old remedies wouldn't work.

After any jolt, the knee would swell, before subsiding a week later. Then it was a case of stretching the knee and the quads, to even out the inflammation. Ensure that the inflammation was not isolated to the knee, get it around the leg, and you don't notice it then. Ice and away I went again.

But it was only a matter of time before that repeated process caught up with me. It already had as I had terrible problems with my left groin for four years. I was on the painkiller, Difene, for three years solid. The problem was that my knee wasn't taking all of the weight now... the groin was. My groin was now compensating for that left knee in terms of running and kicking and there were mornings when I struggled to get out of the bed.

The pain was that intense after training the night before, but Difene became my best friend. Technically, a player can continue to operate with the condition known as Gilmore's Groin, but I underwent surgery in 2004 to cure the problem. It was the fashionable GAA injury at the time and in Mayo we had a spate of Gilmore's Groin problems, with David Heaney, Fergal Kelly and Dillo also nursing similar complaints. People wondered at the time if heavy training schedules were the cause but in my case, it was the knee injury that I had suffered in 2001.

Ultimately, there was no escaping the fact that I had effectively played for a decade with damaged cruciate knee ligaments in my left knee – and I wasn't going to get away with that for much longer. A scan with Ray Moran confirmed that I had torn the medial ligament at training in Jordanstown and that was the only ligament that was left in the joint, holding it together by a thread. Ray's prognosis was stark.

If I took a chance and decided not to undergo surgery, I could be getting out of bed in the morning or exiting the driver's seat of the car and the knee could go. 'It's not a cruciate you'll be getting then,' he warned. 'It's another knee.'

Ray stressed that surgery would give me a better quality of life in later years but football was the big issue as far as I was concerned. It was Horan's first year in charge, there was a feeling of enthusiasm coursing through the county and I didn't want to miss out. But I had to think long-term and after taking a day or two to mull it over, I asked Ray to book me in for surgery.

After making that decision, Mayo's next training session was scheduled for Breaffy House. I told James Horan and his new selector, James Nallen, that I had decided on surgery to fix my knee.

'Ya, grand,' Horan said, as he shrugged and walked away. Nallen was a little bit more forthcoming.

'Grand, Conor... keep in touch.'

On Valentine's Day, February 14, I was operated on at Santry Sports Clinic. I was nervous before the operation but when I woke up from the procedure, I could lift my knee. I fell back to sleep but when I opened my eyes a second time, the pain was incredible.

I was obviously loaded with drugs the first time I awoke. But on that very first day, I was told to walk, because recovery starts there and then, from the minute you exit theatre. I hobbled on a crutch, tensing my leg muscles and realising that this rehabilitation would take a long, long time. But I resolved that if the specialists told me that I'd be back playing in six months, I'd return in four and a half.

If they told me ten months... I'd make it back in eight and a half!

During surgery, part of the patellar tendon, which connects the kneecap to the shinbone, was removed to form a new anterior cruciate ligament. The post-op swelling was massive but my mind was made up. I'd be back for the Mayo club Championship with Shrule and if the county team progressed to the All-Ireland quarter-finals, I'd be involved in that.

Facilities were excellent in Jordanstown and I was soon hitting the gym twice a day, working with Monaghan's Kieran Hughes. Kieran had tendonitis in both knees and had no major experience of strength work before embarking on his own course of rehab.

Marty Loughran, our physio at Jordanstown, oversaw our progress and there was some communication with Liam Moffatt in Mayo. I'd known Liam from DCU, where he gained a degree in athletic training before studying physiotherapy. But that was the extent of the contact from Mayo during the time that I was away from the squad.

In normal circumstances, injured county players would receive significant assistance from the county team. Andy Moran, for example, was very well looked after when he damaged his knee in 2012, but I wasn't. Perhaps it had something to do with the fact that I was injured training in Jordanstown but my original knee injury was sustained while playing Under-21 football for Mayo. Besides, a county player should never feel totally isolated from the squad, even when he suffers a long-term injury.

It's not uncommon – in fact it's pretty much the norm nowadays – for rehabbing players to work on their own individual programmes within the team environment when they're nearing a return to performance. At county sessions, you'll see recovering players using exercise bikes on the side of the pitch or working on their conditioning with a boxing trainer. That didn't happen for me and while it didn't particularly bother me, it still played on my mind. The lack of contact annoyed me more.

It was disrespectful.

Nevertheless, I continued to work hard, twice a day. I really wanted to get back for the summer and I was back jogging six weeks after the operation… very slowly. Some days the knee felt weak, other days not so. The routine was weights twice a day, seven days a week and an ice bath every day. It was all leg work, no upper body. For a spell, it seemed that my life revolved around one-legged squats but Marty assured me that everything was going according to plan.

It was great to have Marty with me but I didn't want him there all of the time either. I asked him for a programme and assured him that I would check with him every few weeks. I wanted to do this my way because a physio won't have you back in four and a half months. He'll aim for six or eight months, erring on the side of safety and caution. Maybe I was wrong, or maybe I was right, but I was back playing club football in early July.

A huge part of that was down to Marty. He could gauge where I was in my recovery on how I was feeling. If I was going too hard, he'd tell me to ease off the gas. Our relationship was based on one hundred per cent honesty. If I felt pain, I'd tell him and he'd prescribe a day's rest.

And that's the most important thing for any player coming back from serious injury – honesty with your physician. He knows the pathway to full fitness, you don't.

It was great to return for Shrule against Claremorris and I managed to convert two late frees to secure a draw. James Nallen was in the stand and it wasn't long before James Horan was commenting on my return. I felt that after working so hard to get back, that another couple of weeks would have me back up to speed for a return to the Mayo squad.

Match fitness was one thing but I felt ready to return to training with the county panel. Horan had other ideas, stating that it could be 'several weeks' before I was welcomed back into the set-up.

'He needs to be playing consistently at club level before he can expect to make the step-up to inter-county fare after an injury like that,' Horan told the *Western People*. That was fair enough… I wasn't expecting to walk straight back into the team.

I had been texting him throughout the summer but the responses from James were short. I was told that they'd keep an eye on my club form but I was ready to train and my knee was stronger now than it had been for a decade. All I wanted was the opportunity to get back in with Mayo but the call never arrived.

That upset me and smacked of more disrespect. Of course it's the manager's prerogative to pick his panel as he sees fit but the least I deserved was an explanation as to why I wasn't back in.

I felt like I was living in limbo land.

I'd trained twice a day for four months to get back playing for my club and county. And I worked hard to the keep the lines of communication open with Horan. When I got back, I continued to send the texts, just to let him know where and when I was playing with the club. I didn't want him to forget about me because when you don't hear anything back, which was often the case, it's easy to think in your own mind that they're moving on without you.

I did fear that that was the case but just because you have an injury doesn't mean that you're finished and that you should be treated like a virtual outcast, when other players that suffered long-term injuries were kept in the fold. Injury can finish some people but it wasn't going to finish me.

And there was no way I was giving up on my Mayo career – and my dream of winning an All-Ireland senior medal – without a fight.

31
CHAPTER

There seems to be a perception out there about the so-called 'super clubs' in Dublin. They're portrayed as opportunistic monsters who plunder helpless rural clubs, robbing them of their best talent.

The reality is far different and in my case, my move to Parnells, based in Coolock in Dublin, was a no-brainer. The transfer from Shrule-Glencorrib was confirmed in November of 2011 and it all happened very quickly. And I approached Parnells... not the other way around.

At home, the quarry business was quiet and there was no work for me. I had to go somewhere and Dublin was the obvious move. From my time there in college, I knew the city and from talking to other players who had been in a similar position, it's where work was to be found.

I'd been sitting at home for six months and the routine was always the same. Get out of bed in the morning, go to the gym, watch TV... and finally go training. That was it... every day. That's all well and good Monday to Friday but I didn't have a pot to p*** in at the weekend.

And you can't keep asking your parents for money at nearly 30 years of age. I was banking on expenses at the end of the month, the mileage allocation for training with Mayo, and that's no way to live.

I knew a couple of lads who played for Parnells and one of them, Colm Begley from Laois also studied at Dublin City University. I was looking for a couple of things from my new club – a friendly atmosphere and a good bunch of players. I eventually met the club chairman, Frank Gleeson and I liked what he was telling me.

Parnells had good players and a clear vision. This was a good fit for me but, naturally, it would be one hell of a wrench leaving Shrule-Glencorrib. My last game for them was a League game against Crossmolina - and the Cross' lads wished me well out on the pitch. Back in our dressing room, I tried to speak to the boys but I couldn't. The enormity of the situation hit me hard and I broke down in tears. I'd played with these guys virtually all of my life and now I couldn't even speak to them. Kenneth and Trevor were in the dressing room and it was Kenneth who broke the ice... calling me a pussy! But it was very tough to leave and I hated doing it.

We had a party the following weekend in the local but I consoled myself with the thought that I wasn't saying goodbye because I'd still get home to Shrule now and again. I told James Horan and the Mayo management team about the move and they were fine about it. No issues there.

Initially I worked as a coach with the club.

Parnells have coaches in the local schools but I knew that a job was becoming available within the club, as a gym manager. There were four or five other candidates but I was confident. My credentials were good as I had a Sports Science degree from DCU and a Masters in sports and business management from University of Ulster, Jordanstown. I was highly-qualified but I wasn't a shoo-in for the job by any means.

At that time, any job that became available was highly sought after and competition was fierce. I'd never really bought into my Dad's old saying some 10 years before, when he said that I'd need a piece of paper to get a job but now I understood why he had said that, and how valuable my studies had been.

I don't get a cent more from the club outside of my weekly wages in that job. Players don't join Parnells for €50,000 a year. We have the best and most famous goalkeeper in the country in Stephen Cluxton and he doesn't receive any financial remuneration whatsoever. Anybody who is paid is employed by the club, which runs as a business. There are 61 employees at Parnells. I'm one of them, so is Begley and the Wexford hurler, Andrew Shore. Begley and Shore are good lads and good friends now. Willie Henry is another guy I've become very friendly with in the club. I get paid my salary, the same as any other employee.

This is the club that I wanted to play for, particularly after sitting down with Frank Gleeson. I had enquired about Ballymun Kickhams, Kilmacud Crokes and St. Sylvester's but Frank, a successful businessman in his own right, is an impressive guy. And the opportunity to sit down and be interviewed for a job excited me. Finally, I could impress upon a potential employer that I possessed the necessary skills to fulfil a role. After six months of sitting on the couch, that felt good. I felt wanted.

The initial adjustment to working life in Dublin was a difficult one, I must admit. A full-time day job is a big responsibility and I'd spent the vast majority of my twenties in college. I had a couple of other jobs when I was younger but they didn't work out. I was too young, immature and unreliable. But now I was ready and at Parnells, they've looked after me brilliantly.

The standard of club football in Dublin is excellent as well. A League game is like a Championship game back home. I'd describe my first year as okay… I had a good 2013 and this year I was again… okay I'd say. It's the consistency in the team that's the problem. On different days we'll field different teams whereas in Mayo, you can be pretty certain that you'll have the same team every week.

One of the best things about Parnells was the support that I received from Frank, Tony Fitzpatrick and Dave Feeney. Tony and Frank were both members of the club's executive, and Dave is still there as General Manager.

I knew that they were there for me but what I won't forget is the individual contact they made. It's easy to assume that somebody is there to support you and there can be comfort in that. But actions speak louder than words and these guys backed me to the hilt. I'd be sensitive enough at times when I'm taken out of my comfort zone. And that comfort zone was Shrule.

That was my home, my safe place, and I always felt protected there. But Dublin's a big place and it can be a lonely place as well. You don't have as many friends in Dublin as you do at home. That stands to reason. But the lads made things easier for me. If I needed a day off work, to go somewhere or to talk to someone, I knew that I had their backing and that was very important.

Because it genuinely was a pretty lonely time for me. It wasn't something that I could talk about in-depth to my friends or other people but I could talk to the lads in the club. Frank, Tony and Dave were great as was the former Dublin Lord Mayor, Royston Brady, who's had his own trials and tribulations. Royston worked as a consultant on the new clubhouse when it was built and was the first General Manager there.

These were people that had seen life, lived it, experienced ups and downs. And when I left the Mayo set-up, that was the lowest point of my life. Of course I'd experienced the loss of family members but on a personal level, outside of family, this was the worst I'd ever been. To have that support network meant a lot to me and when I pull on that Parnells shirt, I'm doing it now not only for my own personal pride and to play football, but for those guys and the respect and support they showed me when I needed it most.

I'll try to repay that as best I can for as long as I can. They're just a good bunch of people. Now, Parnells is not the smoothest run club in the country and there are people within the network who don't help that situation. If they're that worried about the club, why don't they get involved, as opposed to just standing on the side of the pitch, bitching about everything and everybody? Take a team, take a training session, make an effort? Don't come down on a Sunday for a bitching session and then carry it on in a local watering hole.

If someone is worried about a particular team or player then why don't they get involved... coach him, make him a better player and thereby help the team. Do that or don't say anything!

If you have one bad egg within a club, it can destroy the entire basket. Joe Brolly, the former Derry player, had a pop at us this year and that amused me. What gives him the right to comment? People like him don't know what goes on inside a club of the magnitude of Parnells.

Parnells is a genuine GAA club with a business side to it also. The football team is struggling, admittedly, but we don't have our full team each week and some of our players are committed to county teams. The wider issue is that some local people aren't committed enough to the club. It's something I wouldn't have been familiar with back home in Shrule. A different dynamic exists, in that sense.

And so it's unfair for media people to fire pot-shots when they don't know anything about the place.

There's so much more to do in a city. Players have the option of doing other things. In the country, the whole week revolves around a game on a Sunday, and training on Tuesday and Thursday nights. There's no nightclub in Shrule, no cinema, no bowling alley. There is in Galway but that's 20 minutes away. In Dublin, you catch the bus or the Luas and you're in town in minutes. A whole new world opens up.

Pubs, nightclubs, cinemas, live sporting events. There are so many distractions and while I like that, it's never taken away from my main focus, which has always been on training and playing games. I've always lived for that. I work during the day, train in the evenings and play my games at the weekend, irrespective of what's going on in the city.

I can go in there any time I want but I've never lost my drive to be the best that I can be as a player. And that's not going to happen by going to the pub or the cinema on a regular basis. I look after myself and I make sure that I'm present for training and games. I will live like that all of the time until I retire. If I find myself deviating from that path, I'll know the game is up.

I miss Shrule, of course I do.

Family is what I miss most about the place. Mam and Dad are getting a bit older now and I'm conscious of that. Granny is getting older too, and I don't see my nieces and nephews as often as I should. And I don't get home as often as I should either. That preys on my mind but it's almost a three-hour trek and after a long week's work, we might have training or a game with Parnells. And I still can't bring myself to miss training to go home.

I don't have to train, nobody is forcing me to, but it's part of my make-up. And that's why I don't take on board negative comments about myself. I don't let them affect me… why should I? What gives somebody who doesn't know anything about me, or my dedication to football, the right to comment?

I work hard and that's just the way it is… and has to be. It's what my family instilled in me. It's how my brothers trained and you couldn't but be any other way watching them or watching Dillo, Andy Moran, Austy, Chuckie, Brady, McDonald, Heaney, Nallen or Fergal Costello.

The Mayo players I played with, and guys from Shrule I soldiered alongside, always brought that to the table. What's the point otherwise?

And that's why it was hard to leave Mayo, hard to adequately express how I truly felt. If the tears didn't come, I'd have told the Shrule boys in that dressing room… 'Thanks for everything over the years but it's my time to go… I have to go and get work.'

But I just couldn't do it. And yet they all understood, shook my hand and wished me well. I walked out of that dressing room and closed a huge chapter in my life. But when I search deep inside my soul, I know that I gave it all that I could. We were a junior club when I started playing in the adult grade but we jumped to intermediate… then senior, and finally to the high of playing in a county senior final.

And they're still doing ok now… Shrule. They're still competing. I've watched them in a few club games and they have a good squad, with some good young players. Football is life there but, in Parnells, there's a huge struggle to attract young players. O'Tooles, Naomh Mearnóg, St. Vincent's and St. Sylvester's are other GAA clubs in the local catchment area. Hurling and soccer are strong too. I played a bit with Kilmore Celtic and you also have St. Kevin's boys competing for young hearts and minds.

I've notice that parents want to see their young boys playing soccer. They see it as a way out of financial insecurity. If he's a good player, he might go to England? That's the way it works. And so, while we might have some county players in our ranks at Parnells, we have our problems just like any other club.

Our name or perceived financial strength doesn't make us immune in that regard.

CHAPTER 32

AS I reached for my mobile phone to call James Horan, a huge wave of emotion rushed over me.

With tears in my eyes, I punched in the digits and pressed the call button. There was no going back now... I knew it. I was calling time on my county career with Mayo.

It was a beautiful afternoon and I was sitting outside a café in Malahide when Horan put through the original call, informing me that I was not in the team to play Sligo in the 2012 Connacht senior football final.

'Grand,' I said, before hanging up.

When I cooled down, I rang back and told him that I was leaving the squad. The phone conversation, as I recall, lasted for over an hour.

'Jimmy, you don't fancy me.'

I put it to him straight.

'Ah... we do!' he replied.

Jimmy explained his reasoning behind the team selection and he told me that he wanted to come and meet me.

'There's no point, Jimmy.'

It was like a verbal game of tennis. Over and back... over and back. My voice was crackling with emotion.

'I'm not part of your plans. I'm playing well in training and not being picked... I'm not wasting my time travelling up and down every week.'

'We want you there... you're an important member of the panel,' he stated more than once.

The phrases were repeated time and time again.

'Look, Jimmy. I've been doing well in the A v B games and putting up big scores.'

'We're going with this for Sunday,' stated Horan, '... and you'll be coming on.' But it cut no ice. I had a decision to make and I went with it.

Was it the right decision?

Sometimes I wonder, but I had to go with what I felt was right at the time.

James Horan's decision not to pick me had confirmed my suspicions. He didn't rate me as a footballer.

That's the only logical conclusion that I could come to.

I hadn't been picked either for the semi-final victory over Leitrim and by then, I was sick of it all. It was a three-hour drive to and from training and knowing that I wouldn't be playing in the team, no matter how well I was doing in training, sent me into a spiral of near depression.

My mood was desperate in those weeks before I left. My parents commented on it and so did my fiancée, Sara. I was hard to live with. It placed a major strain on our relationship and my mood swings were the primary reason.

I'd spoken to Dillo and Peadar Gardiner after the Leitrim game, explaining to them how I was feeling. I'd come off the bench in that game and scored two points, including a free, and my form in training was really good before the Sligo game.

I expected to start but when Horan made a change in attack, it was Enda

Varley who got the nod ahead of me to replace Alan Freeman.

Horan rang me on the Tuesday before the game to break the news. I'd been weighing up my options after the Leitrim game but Dillo told me to hang in there. Of course I was p****d off.

Players want to play and I was no different. But when James told me that there was no place for me in the starting line-up against Sligo, that was the final straw.

I fought back tears when I rang him back to tell him that I wouldn't be travelling home for training.

'I won't be there tonight,' I said.

'I'm leaving the panel because you've obviously lost faith in me as a player.' James responded by claiming that wasn't the case and he asked to meet me.

But my mind was made up.

That was that, effectively. The news soon got out and the phone went mad. I was painted as a p**** because I had decided to leave just a few days before the Connacht final. But this wasn't just a snap decision.

There were incidents along the way that led to my decision.

When Horan was first appointed I reacted to the news like I had when previous Mayo managers were unveiled. It was exciting.

New manager... fresh start. And Jimmy had done good work with Ballintubber, taking them to a county final. Jimmy had enjoyed a good career too with Mayo, winning three Connacht senior titles and three All Star awards. He played in three All-Ireland finals including replays and scored two points against Kerry in 1997 after coming on as sub.

He was a player I held in high esteem and he was a key member of the team when I made my debut in 2002.

As explained, I hadn't heard from him throughout my entire rehabilitation process. After surgery in February, I returned to action with my club Shrule-Glencorrib in early July and had hoped to make an appearance or two with

Mayo before the end of the season. That didn't happen... we lost the All-Ireland semi-final against Kerry by nine points and my next contact with Jimmy was later in the year, when we met at the Skylon Hotel in Dublin.

I left that meeting worried.

What he'd said needled me.

He talked about how there were good players in the Mayo squad now, the likes of Enda Varley and Jason Doherty. They were the young guns now and I had to come back in to displace them, he informed me.

That was fair enough but I felt that I was a better player than them, and that my statistics as a club footballer backed that up.

Still, I was back with Mayo, which pleased me, and during the early rounds of the 2012 Allianz League, I got back into the swing of things pretty quickly. In six games, including the first game against Dublin that was abandoned due to fog, I scored 0-23, but my best performance of the season came against Dublin in the re-fixed match on March 31.

History was made at McHale Park when I became Mayo's all-time leading scorer. I hit eight points, including three from play, to overtake the great Joe Corcoran. I had now scored 14-380 in 95 League and Championship games for Mayo, with Joe racking up 20-358 during his career.

'When you get older,' I commented to the media, 'It's not really about records any more.' I added that there were 15 men on the field! It really was a good performance and a result that we needed, as we hammered Dublin by 0-20 to 0-8.

A week later, I was left out of the team to play Kerry in Tralee. I came on for Mickey Conroy, but Jimmy told me a few weeks later on a training camp that he had been 'testing' me.

It didn't feel like testing to me... more messing with my mind. Jimmy didn't need to test me. He'd seen me play with Mayo for 10 years.

And he would have seen me playing against Ballintubber in a County Cup final in 2007, when I scored 1-9 against them. Horan knew what I could and couldn't do, so why was he testing me? It was the likes of Varley and Doherty, relative newcomers to the scene, who might have needed testing more than me.

A week after being dropped for the Kerry game, I was back in the team for the League semi-final, against Kerry again. I scored six points in the first half.

We won the game after extra-time but he'd taken me off. In the final against Cork, we lost by 0-11 to 2-9.

I hadn't performed well in the final but that applied to the entire team and the League had been good to us. Coming back from knee reconstruction, I felt that I'd done well, bought into what James wanted me to do, and finished as top scorer. To go from there to not featuring in the Championship was not good enough.

I was told before the Connacht final against Sligo that the full-forward line was picked because they were the best tacklers. But tackling was never a problem for me.

It was a convenient excuse.

I'd never felt like this before with previous Mayo managers. They'd shown faith in me and I was an important cog in the team. I'd read a lot of stuff in newspapers and online, about how the game was evolving, that I was lost and how it was all about working hard now.

But I've always worked hard and the way I saw it, a forward's most important task is to put the ball over the bar.

And I was still doing that, consistently.

The Mayo County Board issued a statement confirming that I had left the squad...

"The Mayo GAA County Board can confirm that due to personal reasons, Conor Mortimer has decided to leave the current Mayo senior football panel. The Management, players and Mayo County Board would like to take this opportunity to thank Conor Mortimer for his services this year to Mayo GAA and indeed for his services throughout the years.

"Conor has been a great servant to Mayo football and his contributions will live long in the hearts of Mayo people.

"We would also like to state the door is always open for any player who is showing the skills, commitment, ability, and passion for Mayo GAA, now and in the future."

That last line annoyed me.

My commitment should never have been called into question. I'd played for the county team for the guts of a decade without a cruciate ligament in my knee and worked like a dog to come back after surgery.

James Horan had frozen me out. He played mind games and they worked. On the Thursday evening before the Sligo game, my family issued a statement to Midwest Radio… our local station in Mayo.

It read as follows:

"Conor lived for Mayo football all his life. He began his inter-county career in the Ted Webb competition and suffered numerous injuries over the years. Both of his brothers, Kenneth and Trevor, played for the county also and suffered injuries like Conor over the years. They are one hundred per cent behind his decision.

"The family feel that Conor, Kenneth and Trevor owe nothing to Mayo football. Conor is a colourful character and made many friends and some enemies over the years while playing.

"Conor was out of football for 12 months last year with a knee injury. The manager James Horan never contacted him to see how he was coming along. When he returned to football, he was playing super football for his club Shrule/Glencorrib. James Horan was notified of a game he would be playing in, but did not attend.

"The family feel that Conor wasn't wanted in the team. Every time Conor was dropped James Horan told him he had a new plan, in that he had found two goal-scoring forwards. However, the Mortimer family feel that plan has not materialised.

"Conor was playing well in A v B games in training of late and two former Mayo managers saw him and can't understand why he wasn't picked. He scored 0-8 against Dublin in the League in Castlebar and was Man of the Match in that game, which was well deserved. He was dropped two weeks later for the Kerry game and only played for 10-15 minutes of it.

"He was dropped again from the starting 15 for the Leitrim game because of this plan referred to by the manager. He is currently fourth choice as a corner forward and it has destroyed his confidence. He wasn't happy with the way football was being played in the Mayo camp.

"When the previous manager was in charge, there were four Shrule-Glencorrib players on the panel. Now there are none. Mark Ronaldson was another example from last season – he was playing well and was dropped from the panel. In the last seven or eight Connacht finals that Mayo were involved in, Conor was top scorer in six of them. He is the all-time leading scorer in Mayo. He feels he has another three years of top-level football in him, but has made his decision and his family are behind him.

"Football was his life and he was never found wanting. He always made himself available to the media, but now all he wants is his privacy and integrity protected.

"His family are extremely happy with his achievements and are very proud of him and have always been 100% behind him and remain so."

My father rang me on the Thursday evening and asked me to tune into Midwest Radio. I had no indication whatsoever that a statement was coming and tuned in via an app on my phone.

I sat in my flat in Saggart and listened to the statement being read out. I might not have agreed with the delivery of the statement but there was little in it that I could argue with. Horan had called me again the previous day, wondering if I had reconsidered my decision to walk away.

I told him that I hadn't. Even if I had, any chance of a comeback or reconciliation ended when that statement was released.

The line that struck me in the statement was the one which opined, "The family feel that Conor wasn't wanted in the team."

I'd never said it to anybody, not even my family, but it was difficult not to think that way. And it's very important for a county player to feel wanted, to feel part of the set-up. I felt nervous before every team selection, when it shouldn't have been like that. My form was good enough to start in every game. When you go to work, you work hard and the rewards should follow.

But no matter what I did in training, I found myself wondering whether I'd be playing or not? And so if Jimmy's aim was to get inside my head, it worked.

The statement didn't help matters but I couldn't criticise my parents for issuing it. They've supported me all of my life but it embarrassed me a little because it came across as if I'd told them to write it. There he is, the little boy running to Mammy and Daddy. But it wasn't like that.

I'd been dealing with the media for 10 years. If I wanted to put something out there, I could have contacted a journalist that I knew. Am I going to criticise my parents for saying what they did? No. They brought me to where I was as a player and they were within their rights to say what they felt at the time.

The media seemed to back Horan and his stance.

I felt isolated, alone and vulnerable. Horan had an army behind him. I had my friends, and Sara was one hundred per cent supportive, but I couldn't expect them to come out and speak on my behalf, like my family had.

Later in the year, I agreed to speak to newspapers before the All-Ireland final. I did… and somehow I was cast as the bad guy?

Now I'm sure many people have said that Horan was right to drop me and they're entitled to that opinion. But people that know me for a long, long time understand what I'm about. Football is very important to me. Always has been… always will be.

Liam McHale, John Maughan and David Brady were three guys who felt that I still had something to offer. Maughan had called me when he heard that I wasn't playing against Leitrim. He couldn't believe it. I'd told him that I was thinking of jacking it in but John told me stick it out.

So I did for a while.

It was an unfortunate episode, when I look back on it now.

I took to Twitter to state: *'Mayo football is bigger than any player always has and always will be so can people just concentrate on getting behind the team for the game on Sunday. I have, even as a player, always been a huge supporter and I will be again this weekend.'*

I texted Enda Varley too, wishing him the very best and urging him to ignore everything that had happened. And even though he didn't pick me, I still have a lot of respect for James Horan.

It would be very easy for me to say… 'f*** him… he s****** me over', but I don't feel that way. He picked a team that he felt would win games. I believed that I should have been in the team and so I left. It's quite straightforward but my career history and profile until that point made the story bigger than it should have been.

The lads in Parnells were top class at the time. They'd been in touch and assured me that if I needed anything, they were there for me. It was nice to hear. But this was something that I had to muddle through for myself.

To a large degree, I internalised the situation.

I watched the Sligo game at home in Saggart... and watching the Mayo games for the remainder of the season was tough.

I was thinking that it should have been me out there, and it remained the very same until James Horan finally stepped down as manager in the summer of 2014. But there was never a part of me that wanted to see Mayo lose.

No way.

Not these guys, some of whom I had soldiered with for a decade. I couldn't think like that, even if I tried. If Mayo won the All-Ireland in 2012, I'd have had mixed emotions. Of course I would. Elation and joy on the one hand for guys like Dillo, Zippy and Aidan O'Shea, the lads I loved togging off with in the dressing room, but a sadness too that I hadn't been involved.

I'd dreamed of winning an All-Ireland with Mayo since I was a young boy and had they finally lifted Sam Maguire, just a couple of months after I'd decided to leave, God knows how that would have felt?

But I couldn't justify staying any longer. I couldn't live with that feeling of exclusion, the mind games, the moods, the driving, the knowing that there were players in the team that I was better than.

It was sad that it ended like that because Jimmy was decent to me when I first joined the Mayo squad in 2002. And when we met first, shortly after his appointment, he asked me if I wanted to play and if I was ready to play? I assured him that I was on both counts.

But when I thought about it further, I guess that Nallen was trying to lay down his own marker... that our relationship had changed and that as a member of the management team, he had to be more stand-offish, I guess.

I'm not sure how much influence any of Horan's selectors had when it came to team selection though. When I left, I was grateful to Cian O'Neill, who was coach with the team, for ringing a couple of times. I always felt that Cian had my back in team selection but he wouldn't have had a huge amount of influence when it came to the big calls.

Of course James Horan was the manager and he always had the final say. But I don't know if he was ever challenged, or questioned, when it came to picking the team.

In spite of everything, I held out hope that something could be done about my situation. And two weeks after the Connacht final, still adamant that there was no way back, I met the team's liaison officer, Noel Howley in a Dublin hotel. I sat with Noel, ate a steak and drank a glass of red wine, and listened to what he had to say.

At the end of our conversation, I agreed to meet with James Horan, to see if we could find some resolution. Noel told me that he would get back to me but I never heard from him after that. I texted him some time later and he said that he was still trying.

I was in touch with Dillo a couple of times too.

Dillo was a Ballintubber clubmate of Horan's.

'Here, Dillo… sort it out,' I had asked.

But I don't think there was any real drive within the Mayo dressing room to get things sorted out. I could have held on and claimed a handy Connacht medal but I'd looked at the bigger picture. And I thought it was b******* from Horan, later in the season, when he stated that I could have got back into the team because Andy Moran got injured.

That was a very easy thing for him to say.

I wasn't going to sit around and wait for one of my teammates to suffer a blow like that. That's a horrible thing to happen to any player. You can't live your life like that, waiting and hoping for a break.

I couldn't anyway.

Sitting on a bench… it's limbo land.

You're hoping that somebody plays s**** so you can get in. That's how every sub on every team in the country feels. Nobody will convince me otherwise. I mean, how else is a sub going to get in?

And when I sat on the bench for that Leitrim game, it felt s***. I didn't feel part of it. I felt alienated and the same applied in training for the two weeks leading up to the next game. When you know you're not going to be on the team, and you're listed on the B team for A v B matches, it's very difficult.

Horan's view was that there were players in front of me who were better. I didn't agree. Especially when I was performing better in training games. It was the principle of the thing. If you play well in A v B games, and you're doing your stuff in training, you should get on the team.

But that wasn't the case.

And that was my problem.

It was an upsetting time, of course it was, but I should have trusted my gut right from the start. The clues were there and I should have picked up on them, listening to the management talking about the full-forward line not doing this or that!

When you're part of a unit with two other guys, you know the criticism is being directed at you. Managers are cute like that. They won't name-check players. They'll talk about lines of the field, but I knew what was going on.

Maybe it's just me but I wouldn't pick my full-forward line based on who are the best tacklers. Of course it's part of a forward's role to track back and make tackles but if you took a straw poll of managers up and down the country, how many would pick their inside forward line based on how well they tackled? There has to be a mixture of tackling ability and scoring power. I'd put the split at 70:30… with scoring ahead of tackling.

The lack of contact during the time that I was injured bugged me too. Any player then, in his right mind, would have suspected that management didn't want him involved. If any player on a county squad gets injured, there should be the odd phone call, just to check in on progress? I would have thought that after the career I'd had until that time, the least I deserved was a phone call when I was trying to get back to fitness.

Agree… or disagree, but that's how I felt at the time.

But ultimately it was those nights driving back from Mayo to Dublin that really got me down. Three-hour journeys… and you know that you're not going to be involved in the Championship, because you've been picked again on the B team in training.

I wasn't sleeping at night and I was depressed during the day. And when you're on the B team, you're an outcast, just there to make up the numbers. It was affecting my life in so many ways. People have asked me why I didn't sit on the bench and suck it up?

I tell them that it's all very well sitting on the bench to keep management and supporters happy but from the minute the game is over, the lull sets in again because you know that inevitably no matter what you do in training for the next few weeks, you won't be getting back in.

It's not like being an Under-10 or Under-12 juvenile player where the emphasis should always be on enjoyment. You're told to forget about the score-line, to enjoy the game… to have fun. But at senior county level, it's all about winning and it's all about playing and doing the best you can for your teammates.

I didn't train five or six days a week just for the hell of it. Many football people would have viewed me as something of a maverick but I always considered myself a team player. I trained hard and by striving to better myself as a player, that could only benefit the team.

Working hard in training is the essence of team, in my book. If you're working hard and players competing for the same position see that, they understand the level that they need to get to. That brings everybody else on. It really shouldn't have mattered that I might have done a few media interviews along the way and earned a few quid for promotional work, because whenever I walked through the gates of McHale Park, the home pitch in Shrule, Parnells, Croke Park… wherever… my focus was absolute.

That applied on a training day or a match day.

Teams and players can trot the *family* line a bit too much. I never felt energy in huddles. That huggy stuff wasn't for me.

I was more focused on what I needed to do. I'd spend a couple of days thinking about the guy I was marking and how I could better him. I'd be on the phone to players who had played against him... searching for weaknesses and asking the questions.

'What's he good at?

'What's he bad at?'

Leadership isn't the lad who stands up in the dressing room and talks b*******. That's not leadership. It's the fella who grabs the game by the scruff of the neck when it's in the melting pot, making that vital tackle or kicking the big score.

For me, leaders were never vocal.

Sure, there were great talkers and guys I listened to but the leaders I looked up to were action men. I captained Parnells in 2014 but I knew in huddles that I was only talking for the sake of it, because that's what captains are supposed to do.

It didn't feel right.

You should never try to be who you're not. Instead, I try to go out on the field and perform as well as I can. Leadership is contributing to the scoreboard and working hard... not talking s****.

It's my job to score and if I'm doing that... I'm being a true leader.

I would have gone back in there with Mayo, if I felt that some common ground could be reached. I had that discussion with Noel Howley but nothing transpired from it.

Dillo hinted that maybe Horan was open to a conversation but it never went further than that. It would have been difficult to return after all that had happened but I would have taken the brunt of it for a week or two and life would have continued.

There have been plenty of examples of players who stepped away and then came back.

I'm two years away from it now and I doubt if I could go back now... even if I was asked. It's two years away from that massive intensity of training and matches. And I'm two years older!

But there's the other side of me that still believes I could do a job. What have the players that Horan deemed better than me done since I left? That's the question I ask myself.

I never wished for one of the lads to play poorly... never. It was very easy for people to say to me that I should have stuck it out, that if I'd been there that the team might have done better. Hindsight is a great thing. Maybe I would have got back in before the end of the season, or maybe I wouldn't.

There were no guarantees. The facts, at the time, stated that I had gone from first choice inside forward to fourth choice.

The majority of people viewed my decision as me being selfish, that I wasn't a team player. But some players set higher standards for themselves and I was one of them. I was on a panel of 30 players but I played to be on the first 15. Nothing changed for the remainder of the summer, even when Andy went down with that injury against Down.

There was never a thought in my mind that it could be an opportunity for me to get back in. I felt sorry for Andy. I knew straight away that it was a cruciate when I watched it. I texted Andy, wishing him well and urging him to recover quickly, but heard nothing back. But that didn't lessen the disappointment that I felt for Andy and the team.

I couldn't deal with the hype that surrounded the semi-final against Dublin, so Sara and I went away on holidays, to the island of Minorca in Spain. We watched the game there as Mayo beat Dublin in a close encounter.

Dublin launched a ferocious second half fightback and David Clarke made a crucial save from Bernard Brogan. A goal then and Mayo were in big trouble but they showed good character to get the job done. I decided not to go to any Mayo game, but I was at Croke Park for the Donegal-Kerry quarter-final and again when Donegal played Cork in the semi-final.

That was okay, but the days before the 2012 final were difficult.

The buzz around Dublin was good. While I like going into the city, having a coffee and meeting a few friends for a chat, I didn't feel that I could do that for the few days leading up to the final... or the couple of days after.

Mayo people were everywhere and while I usually attend every All-Ireland final, I wasn't at Croke Park to watch my own county against Donegal.

People told me to go... to 'get it out of the way.'

But I had no interest in going into a pub listening to someone giving me s***. I didn't mind some of the stuff coming my way on Twitter. I used to react but I'm better now. I tend to ignore it. You learn from your mistakes. I've said a few things on Twitter that I shouldn't have.

But I always found it difficult listening to Mayo people dishing out abuse in person.

'You let your county down... ' and calling me this and that.

In my heart I knew that if I didn't step away, I'd have been undervaluing myself. There are times when it flashed through my mind what it might have been like had I stuck around?

I could have stayed and played against Down in the quarter-final... scored a few points maybe. Another couple against Dublin... perhaps and then line out in an All-Ireland final?

Then it would all have been forgotten about.

But I wouldn't have forgotten it. I'll never forget the endless hours up and down the road, training like mad, not going out... life revolving endlessly around football. I've always made sacrifices to get my game but I found it difficult making those sacrifices and not getting a game.

I wouldn't say I was gutted when Mayo lost the 2012 All-Ireland final. I never felt gutted when I wasn't playing. I wasn't happy they lost the final. I was disappointed for the lads but I would never lower myself to say... 'Well, there you go now Jimmy!'

It was an unfortunate defeat, yet another sorry story for Mayo at Croke Park. Did I think they'd beat Donegal? They had a chance but if Donegal played well, Mayo weren't going to win.

Donegal had a harder run to the final. They beat Kerry and Cork. Mayo beat Dublin... but it was a Dublin that was playing poorly all year.

I'm a firm believer that the best 15 on any given day will win the game.

Donegal had 15 players and we had 15, but they had a couple of players in positions that were better than ours. Mayo had improved but were still lacking what other top counties have... those two or three top class forwards.

That remains the case to this very day.

I texted Dillo and Peadar after the game, as I had before it.

Dillo was hugely disappointed.

He'd been very good up until the final but he didn't play well against Donegal. But it wasn't just Dillo. Other players needed to stand up and be counted. Look at Dublin when they won the All-Ireland in 2011 and 2013!

Bernard Brogan was a stand out player but Paul Flynn contributed, Diarmuid Connolly too, and Kevin McManamon made a huge impact off the bench. We didn't have that depth.

Dillo got no support around him. He spent all day running after Karl Lacey. If the other four or five forwards marked their men and caused their men problems, all Dillo would have to worry about was Lacey. But too often, Lacey got the ball and bombed forward with it.

That was Dillo on the back foot straight away, watching Lacey playing those one-twos and getting forward to support the Donegal attack and midfield. Kevin McLoughlin had a decent game but overall our forwards were poor.

Forwards either have it, or they don't. In the modern game, you see forwards who are big and strong. They get their weights done, they catch the ball and kick it but they can't run, solo or sell a dummy to a defender.

They're footballing robots.

You might not see another forward like Colm Cooper in our lifetime. That traditional, jinky type of corner forward appears to be a dying breed.

Deep down, I miss it.

Of course I do, But I'm a bit older now, more mature. If I was younger, I'd have made a call or two, actively seeking to get back in. I realise public perception is split down the middle pretty much, if not skewed towards those that don't particularly like me.

I'm okay with that. From what I saw and heard at the time, it seemed that the majority of supporters were quite happy that I wasn't there any more. It's a... 'You're better off without him' attitude.

That was down to how I left the dressing room, though of course the fact that I didn't perform in two All-Ireland finals didn't help either. Mayo fans are a demanding bunch.

And that's the way it should be.

I used to think about how it would have been to come back... and kick the winning point in a big game. That thought kicked in when I left and remained when I read and heard how people in Mayo reacted to my departure.

But that's changed now.

I'm at ease with the fact that I'm one of them now... just a supporter, and back where I started.

CHAPTER 33

Shelbourne Football Club boasts a long and illustrious history in domestic soccer in Ireland, and in Europe.

Based at Tolka Park in Dublin, Shelbourne teams of the past have pitted their wits against giants of the game such as Barcelona, Atlético Madrid, Glasgow Rangers, Deportivo La Coruna, Lille and Steaua Bucharest. But relegated from the Premier Division of the League of Ireland in 2013, Shelbourne now find themselves in a period of transition.

I've been working with them since early in 2014, looking to cut my teeth and gain some experience in the world of strength and conditioning.

My role primarily is to take the warm-ups before training and games. And I'm enjoying it immensely. I will be a coach some day. And working with Shelbourne is whetting my appetite for what might lie ahead. Shelbourne remind me of what it was like when I was with Mayo. I'm an important part of a team… and Shelbourne do what they do at a high level.

I watch young players embarking on their careers, going for trials across the water in England, hope bursting through their veins. I was like that once, when I went across to Swansea.

It's an interesting insight into fitness too. The hard work with Shelbourne is done five weeks before the season begins. They key for coaches is to keep it on a plateau throughout the season. County football is different. Slog before and during the National League, training camp pre-Championship, and peaks and troughs during the summer.

My ambition is to become a coach or a selector with a high level team. And my life experience can help with that, I'm sure. A man can have all the qualifications in the world but in my view, he needs to have been at the coalface too as a player. I remember watching a documentary of an American Football player who was asked about sport psychology. The psychologist was speaking and the player sat there, impassively. The psychologist talked about big games... big pressure. When he had finished, the player raised his hand and asked the psychologist, 'Have you ever been there?'

The psychologist replied that he had not.

The player walked out of the room. The point I'm making is that while sports science and associated strands have their place, life experience trumps all of that hands down.

If I can offer a quiet word of advice in the ear of an aspiring young player... then great. But you'd be surprised how many youngsters with a little bit of devilment in them will go on and actually make it at the top level. The reason why they will is simply because they're good enough.

It depends, too, on someone's definition of talent?

There might be a talented 16 or 17 year old player who never got to senior football. The age-old excuses are trotted out... college, drink... women. That's a cop out.

If a player doesn't make it, it's because he's not good enough. Mentality is part of everyone's talent and determines a career path to a large degree. Someone can be sitting in university digs and the lads he's living with might ask if he's going for a pint?

The young man has two choices now... go or don't go?

It's that simple... black and white.

At 17 or 18 years of age, it's very difficult to instil that single-mindedness into a player, unless he has a bit of it growing up. The exceptional ones will play at the highest level, and I refuse to sympathise with those kids who don't make it and the people who talk about them with a misplaced sense of loss.

As a coach, satisfaction is gained from working with the players who apply themselves, who don't get carried away, the ones who never forget where they came from and the friends that helped to shape them along the way.

I ring some of my old Shrule clubmates to this day. It's easy to keep in touch but I also know it's easier for people to portray me as some big shot.

I don't talk to everyone in Shrule, don't get me wrong. I haven't forgotten what some of them said about me when I was younger. Those people still talk to my parents and I'd ask my Mam or Dad, 'What are you doing talking to him or her?'

Time is a healer when you lose football matches but time will never heal that other stuff.

Paul Galvin has his black book in Kerry, in which he lists the names of people who have p***** him off. I don't need a book... it's all in my head.

The hangers-on are in there, the lads who always looked for *this* and *that* when I was a county player... the lads that jumped on my back when I scored that free against Galway in 2006, or the goal in the Connacht final three years later.

Those same lads who abused me after the missed free against Galway in 2002... and after the two All-Ireland finals!

So, when they call me up and look for me to do *something*, to call to *this house* or *that house*, I say no.

I'd travel to the ends of the earth to visit a young kid but I won't do it for men who have f***** me over in the past. I just won't. I'd do anything for my friends and throughout my life, I'd have five or six good friends, excluding family, who I rely on and talk to regularly. That's plenty.

I'm happy now, at peace.

I'm supporting the team, going to matches and mingling with people. I don't have that fear now about people mouthing off. I still wear a cap to games but I'm not as bothered or as paranoid as I was when I got back to going to Mayo games.

I'll still get a few smart remarks, generally from people with a few too many on board.

'Look at that f*****g eejit'… or 'that w*****'.

I used to let that stuff go but it's a bit different now.

If I heard someone say this sort of stuff at a bar in the old days, I'd have walked away. But now I'll go over and ask, 'What's the story… have you a problem?'

I don't care.

For Mayo, I know that I could still do a job.

And I'd love to play, of course I would. But there comes a stage when it's a non-runner, even if the desire is there. I have to start building a career for myself and the Shelbourne gig is a new lease of life. And when I say make a living, I mean a proper living. Not just surviving.

Because that's all I've ever really done. I've just existed from day to day. I'm used to that. If I didn't have a bob, I'd know where to get one. I'll never be badly out of pocket but I know what that's like too. There were days in Jordanstown and at DCU when I didn't have a pot to p*** in.

Those were low days, waiting until Thursday to get 100 quid from a part time job. But that was my fault too.

If I didn't go on the p***, I'd have had that money.

But I got through.

I always did. And it made me strong. I needed to be to get through the weeks and months that followed my decision to walk away from the Mayo squad in 2012. I don't know if this makes sense but I probably regret leaving now, but I don't regret why I left.

I've never spoken to Jimmy since, or had any reason to be in his company or bump into him. I have my own grievances but it's not a personal thing with Jimmy. If a manager doesn't like a player, fine. Move on.

When I watched Mayo in the 2013 All-Ireland final against Dublin, losing again, I felt tense, very tense. I was at Croke Park with Kenneth on that

September afternoon and I was disappointed.

It was the same feeling I'd had when I was 12 or 13 years of age going to watch Mayo... nervous heading into the ground, that feeling of trepidation and feeling the energy from Kenneth.

It was like old times.

'Will we win, Kenneth?'

He wasn't so sure, this time.

They're the days when you'd love to be involved. If I miss anything, it's the calibre of guys I shared a dressing room with. And leaving that bubble, that cocoon, left a void in my life. It took a while to adjust.

I like being incredibly fit and I like having something to aim for every week. But if you don't play county football, you can't aim for those high levels. I one hundred per cent love playing for Parnells but it's just a different level. Your mindset is different as a county footballer, your behaviour too.

In five years time, who knows where I'll be?

Hopefully involved in coaching because I doubt I'll still be playing. I'll be 37 then and happy, please God. Because isn't that what all of us want?

A few little Mortimers running around too, perhaps? But I look forward to peace of mind above all else.

Because I know what it's like to lose that.

EPILOGUE

Mayo's latest quest for Sam ended in August of 2014, when Kerry won a gripping All-Ireland semi-final replay at the Gaelic Grounds in Limerick. And on the night of August 30, James Horan revealed that he was stepping down as team manager.

In the few days that followed the Kerry defeat, the Mayo GAA Twitter feed was almost propagandist in its content. Supporters and players alike were fawning in their praise of Horan and the work that he had done over four seasons.

The Mayo GAA Twitter account happily re-tweeted whatever came its way. I had never seen a defeat *celebrated* in that manner.

The team's sport psychologist, Kieran Shannon, penned a gushing tribute in the *Irish Examiner* newspaper. It all seemed a bit too surreal to me. We had, after all, failed to win the All-Ireland again.

I thought about John Maughan and how he was pilloried, despite leading the county to three All-Ireland finals.

Okay, Mayo lost all three but Horan brought the team to two finals, and lost both. And yet the manner in which Horan was acclaimed and lauded was in stark contrast to Maughan.

John Maughan was slated for putting Pat Holmes on Maurice Fitzgerald during the 1997 All-Ireland final. It was a move that backfired, but Horan wasn't immune in that sense.

Think back to the 2012 All-Ireland final, when Kevin Keane was named at corner back but marked Michael Murphy instead. Ger Cafferky was surely the man for that job and Keane proved in the second half that he was the man for Colm McFadden.

But while Keane was struggling with Murphy, Donegal made hay. Keane was scapegoated and hasn't played too many games since for Mayo. That can't be good for a player and his confidence. Similarly, Cafferky was hung out to dry when he struggled with Kieran Donaghy in the closing stages of the drawn All-Ireland semi-final against Kerry, and the replay that followed.

Ger's a top class player but his form wasn't the greatest in 2014. Kevin Keane is there... he's another full-back, so why didn't Horan give him a go? Horan didn't have to leave Cafferky isolated. He could have put him into corner back for a spell, let him rebuild his confidence and go from there.

My own personal view is that the sky-high opinion of Horan is a little exaggerated.

This is the best Mayo team we've had in years, but is it really the best ever... which is the opinion of some on the various fan forums?

That's over the top.

You can't compare different eras. Whether or not Mayo have missed their chance of All-Ireland glory is a moot point. There's a good team there and they'll keep going and keep trying. I sincerely hope that they get over the line but the chances were there in 2012 and 2013.

Donegal didn't play particularly well in the 2012 All-Ireland final and still got over the line. Same with Dublin a year later!

In that Dublin game, Keith Higgins was left marking Eoghan O'Gara for the final quarter of an hour in the game – despite the fact that O'Gara was playing with a torn hamstring. At the other end of the field, Dublin's Rory

O'Carroll was concussed.

Dublin were effectively playing the game out with 13 players. In that situation, it's not entirely a management call. One of two things should have happened. Zippy should have taken it upon himself to bomb on, knowing that O'Gara was a busted flush. Or one of the other players should have said to Zippy, 'Push on...!' Mistakes were made and yet that's never been discussed in Mayo.

People have questions but they weren't asked and answered. If you lose a game against a team that plays well but you do too, there should be no need for too many complaints. But when there are glaring incidents and decisions that effectively cost Mayo the game, and perhaps an All-Ireland title, questions have to be asked and somebody has to be held accountable.

Four Connacht titles in-a-row during the Horan era was a good achievement but I'd question the quality of the other teams in the province. Leitrim and Sligo are in the doldrums compared to how they once were, while both Roscommon and Galway appear to be in transition but will get stronger.

Of course, the lines are fine and the margins slim. Before the All-Ireland semi-finals in 2014 all of the talk was that it would be a Mayo-Dublin final. Everybody forgot about Kerry and Donegal. Fans will say that Mayo could have beaten Donegal or Dublin but the opposite applies.

The simple fact of the matter is that we fell short again and we have to pick ourselves up... again.

I would agree that the choice of venue for the Kerry All-Ireland semi-final replay was unfair. But with Croke Park out of commission, it was effectively a halfway house for Kerry and Mayo. Okay, Kerry might have played there a few times before but so what?

And let's be honest, we shouldn't have been going to Limerick in the first place. We should have been preparing for an All-Ireland final. With just minutes left in the first Kerry game, we had it in our hands. It was our own fault that we didn't close the game out. Credit to Donaghy and James O'Donoghue for engineering that late goal but it was ours for the taking.

The replay brought more ifs and buts. Robbie Hennelly's late free dropped short and Kerry won in extra-time. The nasty clash of heads involving Cillian O'Connor and Aidan O'Shea cost us dearly – and that wasn't a management issue. It was just unfortunate.

Mayo would struggle without one of those players but with both of them suffering the after-effects, it was a cruel double-blow. O'Shea is a huge player for Mayo. He's big, dominant and physical. And Cillian is now one of the best forwards in the country.

In that regard, Horan built an excellent team that is now challenging consistently at the top. But that's where Mayo should always be – and deserve to be. Despite that semi-final loss, optimism remained high in the county, fuelled by the Twitter machine and the favourable coverage that followed.

But then Mayo shot themselves in the foot again over the appointments process that saw Noel Connelly and Pat Holmes succeed Horan.

A laughing stock again in how we managed that transition.

I read that the County Board studied Kevin McStay's proposal but didn't deem it good enough. What exactly do they want? McStay would have been a good appointment. He would have freshened things up, however Holmes and Connelly will do a good job, I'm sure.

I played with and against Noel for a few years and Pat gave me my break as a young county senior footballer during that memorable summer of 2002.

Mayo football will survive. There's a good group of players there. But this latest affair has led to fresh embarrassment. The County Board and its inner workings have been called into question once again.

But if anyone is to blame, it's the clubs of Mayo.

They had their chance to speak up and do something about the situation but remained silent. We're to blame because I still consider myself a Shrule man. Always have been, always will be. But where are the people who will stand up and ask the hard questions?

I'll always voice my opinion on Twitter and my brother Kenneth, an infrequent user of social media, felt strongly enough about what had happened to air his views too. Will the famine continue with that kind of stuff happening? There's a good chance it will if things don't change.

***

And yet, someday, I do believe that Mayo will get there.

We will lift the Sam Maguire cup and wash away all those years of hurt. And I hope that I'll be there to see it.

Not only will the players involve have deserved it, but so too will the thousands of men who pulled on that shirt since 1951. The men who set out at the start of every year with that dream dancing in their minds. And when it does happen, I'd hope that they won't forget the men who went before them.

Men like Brady, Nallen, Heaney and Dillo. Men like my brothers Kenneth and Trevor. Men like Chuckie, Clarkey, McDonald, Austy and Billy Joe. Men who would go through a brick wall for Mayo football. Those guys all slipped quietly into retirement without fulfilling their dream.

All they ever wanted to do was play for Mayo and win the All-Ireland. I was the same. And when it happens – and it will – they'll still feel part of it.

Because they know what it's all about.

That *One Sunday*.